Naming Ceremonies...

A guide to devising the content and format of a Naming Ceremony

Dorothy Shorne

No part of this publication may be reproduced without prior written permission of the publisher. Ceremonies may be replicated for individual or celebrant use.

Note that Australian English is used in this book, and will vary in places to spelling used in the United States. Some terminology may be unfamiliar to readers outside of Australia.

Recognition is given to the
sharing of ideas and
concepts by fellow
celebrants.

Second Edition printed March 2025
Copyright © Dorothy Shorne
ISBN: 978-0-6482972-9-1

Cover Image: Ruby Tala
Cover Design: Winsome Books

Winsome Books
Adelaide, South Australia

CONTENTS

Why have a Naming Ceremony? 1
Who can be named? 3
The Elements of a Naming Ceremony 5
Ceremony Elements 5
Associated Rituals 10
Godparents, Guardians and Mentors 16
Godparent Advice 17
Wedding Ceremonies Incorporating Namings 19
Special Ceremonies for Special Children 22
Adolescent Ceremonies 24
Other Rituals for Older Children 28
Adoption Ceremony 30
Selected Naming Ceremonies 32
No 1 - Eleanor Veronica 32
No 2 - Briana Annie 38
No 3 - Barnaby Jet 41
No 4 - Abigail Rose 49
No 5 - Jessica Alice 54
No 6 – Roscoe Alaric 60
No 7 – Tamsyn Briony and Sylvia Evelyn 65
No 8 – Zachary Daniel 71
Baptism Ceremony 77
Baptism Ceremony - Jacob Tyrone 79
Naming Certificates 87
Suggested Readings and Verses 91
Organising the Celebration 102
Acknowledgements 104
Also By Dorothy Shorne 105
About the Author 106

Dedicated to my son,
Oliver

If I raised my child again.
If I had my child to raise all over again,
I'd finger paint more, and point the finger less.
I would do less correcting and more connecting.
I'd take my eyes off my watch, and watch with my eyes.
I would care to know less and know to care more.
I'd take more hikes and fly more kites.
I'd stop playing serious, and seriously play.
I would run through more fields and gaze at more stars.
I'd do more hugging and less tugging,
I'd build self-esteem first, and the house later.
I would be firm less often, and affirm much more.
I'd teach less about the love of power,
And more about the power of love.
Diana Loomans

Why have a Naming Ceremony?

I was appointed as a Marriage Celebrant by the Australian Attorney General's Department in 1994. I had only conducted a handful of wedding ceremonies before I received my first request to provide a naming ceremony. I had to research and upskill rapidly, and the ceremonies in this book are some of those that I have developed and performed since then, including for my then infant son.

There is no registration required for a naming celebrant. Anyone can use the information provided in this book in designing a ceremony, for use either as an appointed celebrant, or as a family member. It is a mix-and-match system, whereby any of the rituals can be incorporated with any of the suggested ceremony wording to create something that is relevant to the family and child involved.

The giving of a name is an important rite in any society, for there is the concept that without a name, there is an incomplete personality. A name is thought to bestow personality; just think of the preconceptions that you may have with anyone called Adolf, Jesus, Madonna, Sabrina, etc. These names are imbued with deep and historic meaning and their use implies an assumption of personality and behaviour on the part of the bearer.

Some cultures believe it is unwise to tell a baby's name before it is christened (or named), as the fairies or evil spirits might steal it. With some of the ceremonies I have conducted, the chosen name was kept a secret until the official naming.

Names have historically also implied kinship or even ownership. A name can be an indicator of nationality, religion, clan, and family. A name is the means by which one is identified, and one is classified. Numerologists maintain that the letters comprising your name have an influence on your personality and your destiny.

A religious baptism traditionally has taken place soon after a baby's birth and for good reason. Until relatively recently, many babies died in the period following birth and in the Christian religion that baby could not ascend into heaven unless he or she had been baptised and named within the disciplines of the Church.

Many traditions and customs direct how the name giving of a child is to take place. Each culture will have their own practices and beliefs surrounding this ceremony. Some of these traditions are based in religious belief, and others are customs that arose around cultural understandings, such as the baby not being a complete member of the family until officially named, in whatever form that might take.

Today, our children have a much higher survival rate, and many naming ceremonies coincide with a child's first birthday. It is not uncommon that they occur even later. We may not fear that these children are eternally lost in limbo if they do not have a ceremony, but we still recognise the value of a naming ceremony.

It forms a welcome to our children. It is a recognition of our transition to parenthood, acknowledging the presence of our offspring and their impact on our lives. It is a sharing with our nearest and dearest, and it is the occasion when we bestow the chosen names upon those children. It is a completion of the birthing process and the start of the next stage of development.

Who can be named?

Predominantly, naming ceremonies are held for young children in the first year of their life, or shortly thereafter, but there are various situations in which a celebrant will be called upon to conduct a naming ceremony. That is not the only occasion on which people may be named, or perhaps re-named.

I have performed ceremonies in the following situations:

- Small children, both infants and toddlers;
- Multiple namings on the same occasion, i.e. for siblings, cousins, or close friends;
- Step children within a marriage ceremony, symbolizing family unity by taking on the name of a step parent;
- Adolescents or adults who never had a naming ceremony when younger;
- Adolescents or adults who choose to revoke a given name, and to be known by another;
- A newly separated or divorced woman who chooses to revert to a birth name, or to be known by yet another name; and
- A person (adult) who was being adopted, and was named as a member of that family.

There may be other situations that arise in which a ceremony of this nature is appropriate to address the needs of the parties involved. Ceremonies for adolescents or adults are usually ceremonies of recognition, confirmation, and transition, rather than of welcome. They are all ceremonies of validation that acknowledge the role and place of the person who is named.

Many of my naming ceremonies have been conducted for families in which I previously married the parents. I have subsequently named one or more of their children, becoming the family celebrant. Catching up with family news and events over the years provides both joy and a sense of connection.

Ceremony and ritual is important in our lives. It provides a sense of belonging, security, and continuity, and provides a sense of order in what is sometimes a confusing world. This doesn't just apply to weddings, namings, and funerals, but also to special birthdays, divorces and separations, coming of age, and other events of family significance. Community ceremonies give recognition to events of national significance (i.e. Anzac Day), and provide a vehicle for people coming together with shared emotion, be it joy, grief, or recognition of momentous events.

I hope that using the material provided in this book, you are able to create your own special event and tradition within your family circle.

The Elements of a Naming Ceremony

A Baby Naming Ceremony is simple to compose. Pro forma ceremonies are presented on the following pages for you to consider. There are several elements of the ceremony you can select, none of which are compulsory, and they are clearly explained.

You may like to choose an existing ceremony and amend it to incorporate the relevant names and the sex of your child. You could also blend components of different suggested ceremonies, or you may like to write all or a part of the ceremony yourself. In that case, the examples given will present a guideline as to content and length.

Ceremony Elements

Introduction   This section welcomes the guests and explains the philosophy of the parents in holding a Naming Ceremony for their child. Similarly, the introduction will explain the rationale for an adolescent ceremony, or any of the other forms of naming ceremony mentioned earlier.

Acknowledgments There may be people who are special in the life of the person being named, and who the parents would like to acknowledge. They may be grandparents or other relative, friends, carers, etc. There may even be an acknowledgment of the effort that some guests have made to attend the ceremony, in spite of living some distance away.

Siblings Recognition of older siblings and the important role that they will play in the life of the youngest member of the family. This can be an important section in making siblings feel included in the ceremony and the importance of the day.

Rituals There are various rituals that can be incorporated within the ceremony, and which have significance for the family. Examples are given in the next chapter.

Body Can cover a range of issues, such as the importance of children in society, approaches to child care, and our mutual responsibilities in caring for and setting examples to children.

Naming Ceremonies

Godparents/ Guardians/ Mentors

Parents may like to appoint others to play a role in the life of their child. The terminology selected for those others will be dictated by parental attitude and preference. There is negligible difference in the role that is taken.

Should parents wish these people to become legal guardians in the event of their death or untimely demise, then such an agreement should be prepared with the assistance of a solicitor. Legal guardians may also be appointed as guardians as a part of the Naming Ceremony.

When asking other people to take one of the specified roles in the life of the child, discuss your expectations for that role, if any.

Godparents/Guardians/Mentors can be given certificates as a part of the Ceremony. The parents may also like to consider a small gift as a token of appreciation of the role that these people will play, such as a frame for the certificate, a framed photo, a plant, etc.

The Naming

The chosen names are bestowed upon the child, or the change of name is acknowledged if that is the case. If appropriate, an explanation of the chosen names is also given.

Poems and Readings One or more poems or readings may be included as a part of the ceremony. Examples can be found within this book, but many more will be found online or via your local library. Typically, the celebrant reads the poems or extracts. but either a parent, godparent, or other person may do so. Occasionally, a parent or other friend will write something for the occasion. In that instance, the author should read the poem or words of reflection.

Conclusion Draws the ceremony to a close, and concludes with the signing of the Naming Certificate and the Register.

Toast Not essential, but some parents like to conclude the ceremony with a toast. If this is the case, champagne or other appropriate beverage needs to be available and ready to pour. An option is to charge everyone's glass whilst the certificates are being signed, and then to drink the toast.

If there are other aspects that parents would like included in the ceremony, they can be discussed with the Celebrant. There are elements of ritual that may also be included in the ceremony, and these are discussed in the next section.

Naming Ceremonies

All the suggested ceremonies are non-religious in nature, but parents may request that religious references be included. Typically, this would be included in a blessing, or the naming part of the ceremony. Perhaps a friend or family member can be called upon to deliver such a blessing. A sample baptism ceremony is provided later in this book.

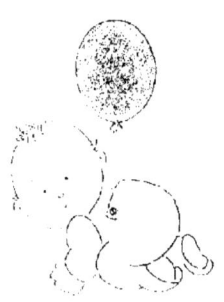

Dorothy Shorne

Associated Rituals

Rituals can be included at various sections of the ceremony, and can either be performed by the celebrant, by the parents, or by others. It is a practical way of including other people in the ceremony. An older sibling may be asked to participate, and this involves them in the ceremony, ensuring that the event is inclusive, and not just focused on the infant.

The following suggestions are some activities you may want to incorporate. The rituals may vary according to the age of the person being named, and the type of ceremony that is planned.

Wish Papers   Wish papers can be given to guests so that they can write their wishes for the child. This can be done on the day, or guests can be asked to write their wishes in advance. They are then collected and read as part of the ceremony. Store them in a memento box for future reference, and reading with the child when he or she is old enough to understand.

Wishes with Coins   Put water into an attractive bowl, preferably non plastic. Guests are asked to bring gold coins for the wishing bowl. The godparents and the child should stand behind the bowl. (Parents show they trust

Naming Ceremonies

the godparents with the child's future by stepping back.)

Celebrant says that the challenges today are many for children etc... so we wish Johnny much for the future. We wish him perseverance and understanding. We wish him good health and compassion. We also wish him good fortune and good humour. The guests are asked to come forward and place their coins in the wishing bowl, adding their own wishes as they do.

When all the wishes have been made, godparents put hands in water, or pour water over hands to 'give' him the wishes of those who love him. God parents then wipe his hands dry and pass the bowl to the parents for safe keeping. The coins then become the foundation of the bank account.

An alternative arrangement is for guests to place the coins in the water on arrival, but the water is still used in distributing the blessings at an appropriate time.

Candle Ceremony

A candle is given to each of the parents to hold, and is then lit. The candle continues to burn whilst a blessing is read for the family. The warmth and light from the candle reflects the warmth of the love that the parents have for this child. If desired, the Godparents may light the candles and read the blessing. (Alternatively, the candles may be given to the godparents to hold.)

A candle decorated with the child's name can be provided, and this is lit as part of the ceremony. Re-lighting the candle on the child's future birthdays becomes a part of family tradition.

Such candles can be purchased from candle artisans, or can be made using instructions easily found online.

Water Blessing Drops of water are sprinkled over the child. A small container of water is required. If the wishes with coins ritual was used as described above, then some of the water imbued with wishes can be used for the water blessing.

Parents who desire a religious element may use the water to mark the baby's forehead in the shape of a cross during the actual naming segment.

With this water, I name you NN. Water is the core of our being and the sustainer of life. As it does a seed in the earth, so may the water nourish this child. May you

Naming Ceremonies

grow tall in spirit, knowing honour and integrity and reflecting wisely on all life choices.

Rose Petal Blessing

Rose Petals are substituted for the water. *With these petals, I name you NN. May life's richest joys and blessings fall upon you as do these petals here today. May you grow in healthy body and mind, and may it be your good fortune to play some worthy part in making life more pleasant for all those with whom you come in contact.*

Parents are requested to supply the rose petals. The sprinkling of rose petals is a suitable activity for an older sibling.

Magic Dust

A light dusting of Magic is sprinkled over the child, whilst words of a charm are spoken. A Godparent can also assist in this ritual.

"With this magic dust, you are empowered to create your own destiny with love, respect, fortitude, and honour. May it bring health, happiness, and good humour."

Initially, I used glitter as 'magic dust' including during my son's ceremony. The glitter caught in the crevices of the pavers and glinted at night when the external lights were turned on, much to his delight.

Look, Mum... magic! We have since learned that the use of glitter in this way is problematic for the environment. There are substitutes if you search on the internet, not all of them suitable for this purpose. The best is to colour some granulated sugar, and use a sprinkling of that. It does not need to be coloured if you don't want to go to that trouble. Any sugar left at the end of the day will easily wash off in the bath.

Tree Planting A tree may be planted within the ceremony. The hole should be dug in advance, and the tree, gardening implements and the tree or shrub should be positioned where required. If there is not an appropriate garden, a large garden pot can receive the plant until it can be transferred to a more permanent home.

Soil from the family homes of each parent could be mixed and used to bed down the plant, symbolising the union of the families in the creation of the child to be named.

Burying the Placenta Some cultures will keep the placenta after the birth of a child, and it will be buried at the base of a tree. The placenta nourishes the tree, and that tree is thereafter known as the child's tree.

Time Capsule	A time capsule can be created using lengths of plastic drainage pipe with caps at either end. Items stored inside should be stored in plastic bags or containers. Typically, items may include newspapers of the day, the child's hand print or foot print, coins, wish papers, and other memorabilia. If buried within the ceremony, the hole should be prepared in advance, to minimise the time required within the actual event.
Anointing with Oils	Essential oils can be selected according to their given properties. They would be mixed with a carrier oil, such as Almond Oil, and would be dabbed lightly on the palms of the hands or the soles of the feet.

This is not an exclusive list of rituals. Others can be devised in consultation between the celebrant and the parents to meet a specific need. There will be examples in the following pages showing their application.

Godparents or siblings can assist with many of the rituals. The godparents often appreciate being given a specific role within the ceremony, and when such a lot of attention is being given to the newcomer, as mentioned earlier, the siblings like to feel that they are important too.

Dorothy Shorne

Godparents, Guardians and Mentors

Before appointing friends or relatives to act in any of these roles, you should explain your expectations to them. If you wish the appointees to become legal guardians for your child, you should consult your solicitor about including this intention in your will.

It is sensible to consider how you would like your child to be raised in the event of your untimely death. These are some sample issues:

- How would you like your estate invested, and when should it be made available to the child?
- Where would you like your child to be educated?
- Do you want funds from your estate to be made available for extra-curricular activities such as music lessons, art classes, dance classes, etc?
- Which people should have visitation rights to the child, and with whom should the child spend school holidays?

You may like to appoint one person as Guardian, because you know that he or she will invest your money wisely for the child's future, and appoint another because you know that he or she has a good understanding of how you would like your child to be raised. The following is an example of the explanation that I gave to the Godparents of my son.

Godparent Advice

The role of godparents is flexible and loosely defined by today's practices. Oliver has been fortunate to have had many people take an interest in his welfare to date, and in that regard, he has a broad network of aunties and uncles. Living as he does in a single-parent household, other relationships that have been forged with Oliver have been most important to his development and wellbeing.

You have been asked to accept the role of Godparent to Oliver. This is not meant to be an onerous or obligatory task. I have asked two people to be Godmother and two people to be Godfather, all of whom have given support and friendship over the years, and who, with their partners, have welcomed Oliver into their lives.

Role models are crucial in any child's life. The nearest models as one might expect are a child's parents, but it is just as important that there are others to whom a child might look for guidance. Godparents can have an important role to play in this respect - not necessarily now, and not necessarily all the time. I see the role of godparenting as being dynamic, robust, and flexible.

I ask that you always welcome Oliver if he comes to you for company, advice or help and that you will listen to him and respect his confidences no matter how great or small. I also ask that you show him understanding and love and let him know he can be secure in his trust in you.

Should I, through some accident or illness, not be around to be with my son through his formative years, my sisters will become his legal guardians. Their guardianship will in no way diminish any relationship that you may have with my son and your continued contact with him would be facilitated.

I thank you for your interest and support, both for Oliver and for myself.

Sample Godparent Certificate, also available for Guardians and Mentors.

Wedding Ceremonies Incorporating Namings

Some families incorporate the naming of their child within their wedding ceremony. The naming usually follows the declaration of the parents as 'husband and wife' and is shorter than a naming ceremony in isolation.

Godparents or Guardians may be appointed, and there can be readings, and other rituals commonly associated with namings. The length of the complete ceremony will be influenced by the age and ability of the child to stay focused and compliant. Naming and Godparent Certificates are also issued.

A choice needs to be made whether to sign the Marriage Certificates and then move into the Naming Ceremony, or whether to transition from one ceremony into the other, signing all certificates at the end.

On the assumption that a woman is changing her family name to that of her partner (not always the case), a brief naming within a marriage ceremony might also occur if a man marries a woman who already has children by another relationship. As a part of the ceremony, he acknowledges the child as part of the new family unit, and can agree to share his family name with his new step child.

Of course, this is discussed with the child (if of an appropriate age) before the ceremony, and is done with the agreement of all parties. Should the situation be reversed, and the new family are all adopting the woman's name, the ceremony can be adapted accordingly.

A Certificate of Family Unity can be issued to the family. This certificate is also signed by the child if he or she can write. It may be a very 'ill-formed' signature, but that is fine. Some step parents also give a small gift to the child as a token of their commitment to each other.

Typical wording that is used within such a marriage is as follows:

> There is a child who will share in this marriage. The formalising of this new family will deeply influence their lives. For everyone involved, including the extended family, it will both complicate and enrich their lives. They will also have much to contribute to this new family. This ceremony therefore, marks not only the union of James and Briony; it also celebrates the beginning of a new family as James joins Briony and her daughter, Gaynor.
>
> James, have you given serious and unhurried consideration to your role and responsibility to this family, and do you agree to share your name with Gaynor? *I do.*
>
> Gaynor, do you give your support to James in this marriage with your mother? *I do.* Are you happy to take on the name of Smith from this day forward? *Yes.* On that basis, you shall henceforth be known as Gaynor Elizabeth Morton Smith.

Naming Ceremonies

Certificate of Family Unity

I, Dorothy Anne Shorne
hereby certify that I have this day
At Para Hills Bowling Club, Para Hills, South Australia
duly presided over the ceremony of Family Unity

between Raymond Martin Evatt and Diana Julie Glasson
and their daughters, Rebecca, Brooke & Bianca

Dated this Seventeenth day of April 2003

Richard .... Deborah ....
Rebecca .... Brooke ....
Bianca .... Celebrant ....

Holly Susannah with Parents and Godmothers

Dorothy Shorne

Special Ceremonies for Special Children

Some children are very ill after birth, or sadly do not survive the birthing process. Ceremonies can be held for these children as well, and a selection of readings are also available to suit different occasions. No matter how short their stay with us, these children are always an important part of the family.

One ceremonial option is to plant a tree, which will give a lasting connection with the child over the years. Guests could be asked to write down their thoughts and wishes for the child, which after being read, are soaked in water, and planted under the tree. A candle bearing the child's names can be lit with an appropriate blessing.

On some sad occasions, I have conducted funerals for babies, and after consultation with the parents, I have conducted a naming ceremony at the beginning of proceedings. Sometimes, I have moved my position within the venue to provide a sense of separation between the two ceremony components. It is important that the child who has not survived the birthing process or infancy, is still acknowledged as a member of their family and community.

Naming Ceremonies

Thankfulness for a special child
For the joy of summer sunrise
And refreshing drops of rain
We are thankful

For the gift of each new morning
And the chance to try again
We are thankful

For a child who smiles like sunshine
And whose cuddles conquer pain
We are thankful

For life's harmonies and discords
For life's comfort and its strain
We are thankful

For this child who brought fresh feelings
And new reasons for each day
We are thankful

For his eyes that speak with meaning
That mere words cannot convey
We are thankful

For the hours and the minutes
And the seconds of each day
We are thankful

For friends' smiles and warming handshakes
When they don't know what to say
We are thankful

For the strength of love here present
May it never fade away.
We are thankful for all of these things.
© Jim Boswell Oct 97

Dorothy Shorne

Adolescent Ceremonies

An older child can participate in the ceremony to a degree not possible with a baby or toddler and the ceremony should reflect this situation. If the child is older, it can still be loosely structured as a Naming Ceremony, but the readings selected would be different. The relationship between godparent and child can be explained, and the child can agree to the relationship as a part of the ceremony.

The ceremony for an older child would be structured more as an **Adolescent Ceremony**. Each ceremony can be crafted to reflect the needs of the child and their stage of development, and as such each will be different.

It can be acknowledged that the child is leaving infancy behind, and is entering the years of the student; learning about life, learning the ways of the family, learning about new responsibilities, and, of course, learning at school. The child is an integral part of the family unit, and this is an opportunity to reinforce this role and sense of identity.

Whether the child is younger or older, it may be appropriate to include the following stages in the ceremony:

- *Releasing* behaviours of childhood,
- *Seeking* new patterns and acceptance,
- *Embracing* new responsibilities and roles.

Release something that typifies childhood. Agreement could be reached to abandon a childish behaviour (e.g. sleeping with the light on at night) or to give up an object that has been clung to since infancy. This object(s) can be given away, or burned/buried. Other objects, memories of childhood, may be carefully wrapped and put away in a memory box, and kept for future reference if they are needed. In releasing a behaviour, the child needs to feel ready, and to understand that there are benefits in doing so.

Children are constantly *seeking* definition of their role within the family, with their friends and within society in general. In some other cultures or societies, there is a time when children leave the family unit for a while to undergo a period of learning and studying, before returning with their new found status and understandings, part of which involves respect for family, for family values, and for the world around them.

In Hindu and other religions, at around eight a boy goes through a ceremony that is a symbolic 'second birth'. It is the beginning of the student stage of their life. A change of clothing occurs during the ceremony. Acknowledging respect for family and elders is an important part of this stage of life.

The rituals of the monastery, or explorations of the desert etc. are not entirely appropriate or feasible for the modern western child, but it is still possible that in the time before the ceremony, there is an opportunity for the child to have a weekend or at least a day away from the family home (and away from television, the computer, and the games console) and has the opportunity to develop new resources, visit new places, and to learn new skills. Most importantly, there should be the opportunity to talk.

This could take place with Mum or Dad, with a prospective godparent, with an aunt or uncle, or some other trusted adult, and preferably would not involve other siblings or children. This is a period of transition for the particular child, and will be seen by him or her as more important if it is not shared with the others. It could be a:

- Camping trip
- Fishing expedition
- Volunteering help at a local soup kitchen
- Helping in a local environmental project.
- A biking or hiking expedition.

The object of the exercise is to involve the child in planning and preparation, and to perhaps learn and think about other children and people in the world, and how we all fit in together (*Seeking new patterns*). Some children have less, other children have more, but they will all progressively assume some responsibility for the world around them and how they interact with their environment and the people in it. The children are of an age where they can start to learn that what they do also impacts on others, and that they can make a difference with constructive behaviours.

This is meant to be a gentle and enjoyable learning exercise, and of course one of sharing between child and adult. It is the opportunity to talk together, and discuss the issues in an uninterrupted and non-judgmental environment. If it is not possible to get away, perhaps the child can be assisted in a project to learn more about how other children live in the world – in other countries, in other religions, in refugee camps, etc. Information is available in newspapers and magazines, at the library and on the internet.

Naming Ceremonies

As a part of the ceremony, the child might be asked what they have learned from this exercise. Alternatively, it may be considered that what has been learnt or experienced is a purely private matter.

Embracing new roles and responsibilities is an important part of growing up. There can be a symbolic gift to acknowledge this new phase in the child's life, such as a new item of clothing, a journal in which he or she can record their thoughts, their own email account, or new privileges such as a later time for going to bed, or something else that the parent knows has long been desired.

Perhaps now is the time to start providing pocket money. With those privileges however come new responsibilities such as household chores, a commitment to only visit web sites that are approved by the parent, or an understanding of the need to share resources within the family. These options will vary from family to family, and can be decided upon after some discussion.

It is possible also that parents can briefly speak within the ceremony, choosing this time to tell the child that he or she is an important member of the family, describing what attributes that they really like about the child, and giving the child positive affirmations and perhaps touching on hopes for the future. The parents can also choose to make this a private communication.

❈

Dorothy Shorne

Other Rituals for Older Children

The gift of a tree may be appropriate for a young girl. It grows with her, matures, blossoms, and bears fruit. There are parallels that can be explored between the maturing and development of the tree, and the maturing and development of the girl. If the family are not living in a permanent situation, there are many trees that can be grown successfully in large pots. Ask the nursery for advice. Preferably, the tree will be of a variety that matures and bears fruit within a few years. A plant or tree can also be appropriate for a boy.

The young person can select an object from childhood to be carried through transition to the next phase. Just as there is meaning to taking leave of the objects of early childhood, there can also be value in recognising what has been and will continue to be important to the child in their future life.

Guests who attend the ceremony can be asked in advance to write their words of advice, wishes, or future hopes for the child. These can be read out as part of the ceremony, and then collected up and kept in an album or memory box. In one ceremony I conducted the children (siblings) were given cloaks to wear, and guests pinned the notes bearing their written words to the cloaks.

If an older child wishes to contribute to the ceremony in any way, this option should also be explored. This contribution could be reading a poem, or something that the child has written.

Naming Ceremonies

Perhaps he or she would like to give guests a 'show and tell' involving a project of interest, or just may be inspired to speak about what the day means to him or her. Whereas there should be no obligation to participate in this way, there should be every encouragement if this is what the child would like to do.

These ceremonies can be a social gathering, involving numbers of family and friends, or can be a more intimate occasion with immediate family. Even if it is just a small intimate affair, the occasion should involve the sharing of a special meal. After all, what is a special celebration without the food to go with it? The child can be involved in the menu planning and perhaps the preparation.

Children today are more sophisticated and self-assured than ever before, making their parents, at the same age, seem quite gauche and naïve by comparison. Nevertheless, it is an unsure world that they are inheriting, and children can be very uncertain of just where they fit into the overall scheme of things.

The answer to this question is one that they must discover for themselves, but this task is so much easier if they can undertake their quest, knowing they have a rightful role in their family unit. Whether that family is the traditional married couple with two children and a dog is not important – what is important though is that the child is secure in the love and support of those who are nearest and dearest. A naming or an adolescent ceremony is one of the many avenues of establishing and reinforcing that sense of identity.

Adoption Ceremony

Adoption may involve bringing a baby into the family unit, or possibly an older child. The child may also have been born in another country.

A ceremony involving an adopted baby will essentially be no different to that of a birth child, except that this is a child who has been chosen by the parents. We welcome and embrace the child in the same fashion, and name him or her with the chosen names. If the child comes to the family with names already given by the birth mother, then those names can be affirmed and combined with the new family name. If new names are to be chosen and bestowed, perhaps the original name can be retained as a second name.

It may be appropriate to acknowledge the role of the relinquishing mother or parents, and to promise that where possible, the child will be brought up with an understanding of his or her cultural background, both through birth and by adoption.

When a child is older, the format of the ceremony may vary and can involve the child directly. Given that there will be a degree of culture shock and dis-orientation for the child on first joining his or her new family, it may be appropriate to defer the ceremony until family members have adjusted and are comfortable with each other.

If there are other siblings, the ceremony can also become one of family unity, in which all members of the family acknowledge

Naming Ceremonies

their relationships and responsibilities to each other. The language used should be age appropriate. A certificate of Family Unity is available, and this certificate can be signed by all members of the family. Those who cannot write can mark the certificate with a finger print, using a brightly coloured stamp pad.

As a part of the ceremony, an appropriately sized memorabilia box should be purchased that can hold a range of treasures. Guests may choose to bring a sizable gift, but they should be asked to bring a smaller token gift. This gift could be a special coin, a trading game card, a stone or crystal, a photo, or small toy. As part of the ceremony, either the child carries around the box, or one by one the adults come forward, deposit their gift in the box, and says word to the effect of:

> 'NN, I welcome you today and offer you this gift. This photo was taken the first day I met you, and I give it to you now so that you may look back later and remember who you were when you came to us.'

The wording, of course, will vary with the nature of the gift. The box will soon contain a range of treasures that provide both a sense of history and a sense of welcome and belonging for the child. It is stressed that these are not meant to be expensive gifts – rather symbols that will be relevant and meaningful for a child.

The rest of the ceremony can be an adaptation from any of the suggested naming ceremonies.

Dorothy Shorne

Selected Naming Ceremonies

Examples of different ceremonies are provided on the following pages. Take ideas from these, or mix and match. The suggestions given may stimulate ideas of your own. In a couple of instances, I have not included the words of the verse that was used. This is because the work is still under copyright, and I do not have permission to reprint it here.

No 1 - Eleanor Veronica

On arrival, guests are invited to drop their coins into the bowl of water and to make a wish. This continues until the ceremony begins. They also place their time-capsule offering into the treasure chest.

Rae formally welcomes her and Lizzie's guests.

Family and friends - my name is Dorothy Shorne and I have been asked to officiate on this special occasion. *Rae* feels enormous pride and joy in the recent arrival of her daughter *Eleanor* and is taking this opportunity to formally introduce her to you, her friends and family, and to bestow upon her daughter her chosen names. Your presence in issuing a welcome to this little person is an important part of the day, and a way in which you can share in the joy expressed by *Rae*.

Rae has undertaken to nurture this child, to love her, provide her with a safe and secure environment, with stimulation, and with guidance as she plots her own course though life. *Eleanor* is an individual, and as such her future life path will be uniquely hers.

Naming Ceremonies

Rae will be there for her throughout, to love and support her, however and whenever she needs it.

Mixed with the happiness that *Rae* has, is also a certain awe at the responsibility that is now hers. This welcome to *Eleanor* will remind her that from now on much of her life will be involved in caring for her. *Rae* feels strongly that the more love this child receives, the more *Ellie* will benefit in life, and the more love *Ellie* can give to others. The more people to whom this child relates, the more balanced and richer her growth will be. So, your presence at this celebration today is appreciated, as will be your interest and involvement in the years ahead.

There are many paths in this world and each individual must find their own. This understanding is reflected in the following words, written by Bryce Courtenay and read today by Jaquie.

> ***A Recipe for Dreaming (adapted)***
> *Verse read here*
> *Bryce Courtney*

Children are a social responsibility. Many of us here are possibly not parents, but we are aunts and uncles, neighbours, and friends. In a myriad of little ways and by example, we are all teachers and mentors. The rewards are not always immediate or obvious, but like all long-term investments, the initial input of time, patience, understanding and caring example will give an ultimate return of a balanced and responsible human being - plus lots of joyful moments as interest along the way!

You are all invited and encouraged to present to *Eleanor* as she grows up, a broad and balanced view of life, and despite religious and cultural differences, to embrace the common virtues of integrity, honesty, fairness and concern, and love towards all people.

Acknowledging that a child needs the support of many people in his or her life, and that parents for a variety of reasons are not always able to be there, *Rae* has asked *Adrian M, Diane P, Julie O, Jade W.* and *Milton T,* all to be godparents to *Eleanor.* Godparents provide love and support for a child, can be available when the parents cannot, or can be available when the child chooses. It is a unique relationship, sometimes bound by blood and sometimes not, but it acknowledges the role that we all play in nurturing the next generation.

Adrian, Diane, Julie, Jade & Milton - Rae asks that you always welcome *Eleanor* if she comes to you for company, advice or help and that you will listen to her and respect her confidences no matter how great or small. *Rae* asks that you show *Eleanor* understanding and love and let her know she will always have a special place in your heart.

Are you willing to accept this responsibility of being a godparent to *Ellie*?

Godparents: We are.

When you arrived, and before this ceremony began, you each placed gold coins in the bowl of water as directed, and made a wish for *Ellie's* future. That water is now imbued with your collective wishes. I now invite the godparents, one by one, to sprinkle some of this water over *Ellie's* hands, and whilst doing so to deliver their own personal wish for her and her future journey.

Adrian: *Ellie*, I wish for you the capacity for a fun and constructive outlook on life, to not let those unimportant things get you down, and to consider those less fortunate.

Diane: I wish for you empathy and understanding, so that you may appreciate your good fortune in life, and may extend a helping hand for those in need.

Julie: I wish that you come to know and love the people that surround you, your mum's friends - us, and that we are always ones who you can rely on to teach, help, love and amuse you

Jade: I wish that you will understand how lucky you are to be happy, healthy, and safe, and to know how to make the right decisions to stay that way.

Milton: I wish that you will enjoy a life of balance and harmony–full of adventures and fun but tempered with the wisdom to make the most of every opportunity in a way that empowers yourself and those around you.

(A godparent to dry *Ellie's* hands with small towel.)

The wishing bowl and coins will be put aside for safekeeping and those coins, donated by you all, will become the foundation of *Ellie's* bank account. On behalf of both *Rae* and *Ellie*, I thank you for your generosity and for your supportive thoughts and wishes. Both actions embrace this young lady and provide for her in the coming years.

Rae – please light your daughter's naming candle. (*Candle is lit*) The light and warmth from this candle is symbolic of the warmth of your love for your child, and the growing bond between you. Each year at this time, you can relight this candle, and as the years pass, and the candle becomes shorter, the love that is expressed in the candlelight about you now will become stronger.

Dorothy Shorne

We now bestow upon you the names of *Eleanor Veronica*. We welcome you, and hope that you will wear your name with pride, joy, and strength. May you bring delight to your mother, your godparents, and to your family and friends. May you join us in striving to make this world a better and happier place

Although we bring them into this world, children are individuals in their own right, and with our guidance, must make their own way on life's journey. The following poem by Kahlil Gibran explains what I mean.

Children
Your children are not your children.
They are the sons and daughters of life's longing for itself.
They come through you but not from you,
And though they are with you, yet they belong not to you.
You may give them your love but not your thoughts,
For they have their own thoughts.
You may house their bodies but not their souls,
For their souls dwell in the house of tomorrow,
Which you cannot visit, not even in your dreams.
You may strive to be like them, but seek not to make them like you.
For life goes not backward nor tarries with yesterday.
You are the bows from which your children
as living arrows are sent forth.
The archer sees the mark on the path of the infinite,
And he bends you with his might that his arrows may go swift and far.
Let your bending in the archer's hand be for gladness;
For as he loves the arrow that flies,
So he loves also the bow that is stable.
      Kahlil Gibran

On behalf of everyone present, I congratulate *Rae*, the mother of *Eleanor* and also the God parents: *Milton, Julie, Diane, Adrian & Jade*. This ceremony today has been meant to strengthen the affection and friendship we all have for each other, but especially the relationship now established by *Eleanor* with all of you. May you all benefit from our involvement with this child and with each other.

We will conclude this ceremony by signing the Name Giving Certificate, after which we will drink a toast to this young lady. Whilst the signing is underway, I invite you all to charge your glasses.

Toast

Eleanor Veronica— ***may life's richest joys and blessings be yours.*** *We wish you good fortune, health and peace on your journey through life. May you find love and comfort when you are troubled, may you find true friendship as you grow and may you learn to be kind and considerate to everyone you meet over a long and happy life. To Eleanor!*

Dorothy Shorne

No 2 - Briana Annie

Family and friends - my name is Dorothy Shorne and I have been asked to officiate on this special occasion. *Dawn* and *Jake* feel pride and joy in the recent arrival of their daughter *Briana* and take this opportunity to formally introduce her to you their family and friends, and to bestow upon their daughter her chosen names. Your presence in issuing a welcome to this little person is an important part of the day, and a way in which you can share in the joy expressed by *Dawn* and *Jake*.

There are many words of advice that one could pass on to a new comer who is at the beginning of life's journey. I have a poster which says in part, "If I had my life to live over, I would pick more daisies." *Briana*, my advice to you is - pick lots of daisies in this life! Make the most of each opportunity and live life to the fullest. There is a poem from the Sanskrit which illustrates this philosophy: -

> *Look to this day,*
> *For it is life, the very life of life.*
> *In its brief course lie all the*
> *Varieties and realities of your existence:*
> *The bliss of growth,*
> *The glory of action,*
> *The splendour of beauty;*
> *For yesterday is but a dream*
> *And tomorrow is only a vision,*
> *But today well lived makes*
> *Every yesterday a dream of happiness,*
> *And every tomorrow a vision of hope.*
> *Look well therefore to this day!*
> *Such is the salutation of the dawn.*

From the Sanskrit   *Naming Ceremonies*

I would expand on this advice by recommending that in everything you do, do it in consideration of and with respect for the rights of others. You are too young now to understand these sentiments, but with love and caring and through example, your parents will explain to you the difference between right and wrong, the concept of sharing, and the meaning of love. They will also support you as you learn to laugh, to grow, to look, to listen, and to learn. It is an enormous responsibility for them, but a joyous task as well.

Children are a social responsibility. Many of us here are possibly not parents, but we are aunts and uncles, neighbours, and friends. In a myriad of little ways, and by example, we are all teachers and mentors. The rewards are not always immediate or obvious, but like all long-term investments, the initial input of time, patience, understanding and caring example will give an ultimate return of a balanced and responsible human being - plus with a few warm fuzzy feelings as interest along the way!

Dawn and *Jake* are helped in this respect by *Briana's* grandparents, and also the guardians that they have selected. Theirs is a special task. They promise to take a lifelong interest in the welfare of the child, and to assume a more than ordinary responsibility in the event of the death or default of the parents. They will also be important role models for this young child.

Dawn and *Jake* ask that you always welcome *Briana* if she comes to you for company, advice or help and that you will listen to her and respect her confidences, no matter how great or small. They ask that you show her understanding and love and let her know that she will always have a special place in your hearts.

I now ask those guardians, are you *Gina, Faye* and *Makon* willing to accept this special privilege?

Guardians: We are.

Parents are given the candles -light the candles.

The light and warmth from these candles is symbolic of the warmth of your love for your child, and the growing bond between you. Each year at this time, you can relight these same candles, and as the years pass, and the candles become shorter, the love that is expressed in the candlelight about you now will become stronger. May the coming years bless you all with good health, with happiness, and with an appreciation always of your good fortune in each other.

We now bestow upon you the names of *Briana Annie*. We wish you long life and happiness in a loving and secure world. May you bring joy to your parents, your guardians, your grandparents, and to all of us, your family and friends. May you contribute to making this world a better and happier place.

You may now blow out the candles.

On behalf of everyone here, I welcome *Briana*, and congratulate *Dawn* and *Jake*, her parents, and also the guardians *Gina, Faye* and *Makon*.

This ceremony today has been held in recognition of the importance of marking the special events in our lives, to witness the giving of a name, and in honour of the newcomer amongst us. May we all benefit from our involvement with this child and with each other.

No 3 - Barnaby Jet

Family & Friends – I welcome you to this place of ceremony. *Gail* and *Alison* – this is a special rite that we share today, and which has importance for all present. We acknowledge firstly your child *Barnaby* and wish him well for the great journey that he has ahead of him. Secondly, we give your child his names in this ceremony. In this act we declare that he is an individual, a unique and separate person with a dignity and life of his own.

Your child was born of your love for each other, and through him, you are led into the future. He goes with the support and wisdom of his family on both sides of the globe, and the role of grandparents and the elders in his life is welcomed. These people provide the strength and the certainty of the past, and support you both as well as helping to guide your child.

Addressing the guests:

You are here because of your relationship with this child and his parents, for you *are* their community—their circle of people. You are the community with whom they celebrate life's special moments, and to whom they will turn in times of need. You are their extended family and friends and in today's ceremony we honour *Gail* and *Alison's* commitment to their son, and also acknowledge with gratitude the role that you all play in the lives of this family. Cousins are becoming a rarer commodity these days, but Barnaby is fortunate to have cousin Erika in Australia. No doubt the children will form a bond which will last through the years to come.

We delight in the arrival of each new child, but as the years pass it is too easy to take our children for granted. Whatever their ages they deserve the tender love and firm guidance, which only we as parents, teachers and friends can give. Moreover, these

Dorothy Shorne

children have a right to a faith in themselves, in the story of mankind, in their particular heritage which is both English and Australian, and in the vast universe-home which is theirs.

It is to symbolize these possibilities and responsibilities that we have come to this ceremony. An important role in the life of any child is that taken by the grandparents and we acknowledge the influence of Barbara and Bernard here in Australia and Francis and Victoria in the UK. I now invite Bernard to come forward and read the poem *If* by Rudyard Kipling. This same poem will also be read by Francis at the English ceremony for *Barnaby*.

> *If - by Rudyard Kipling:*
> *If you can keep your head when all about you*
> *Are losing theirs and blaming it on you;*
> *If you can trust yourself when all men doubt you,*
> *But make allowance for their doubting too;*
> *If you can wait and not be tired by waiting;*
> *Or, being lied about, don't deal in lies,*
> *Or, being hated, don't give way to hating;*
> *And yet don't look too good, nor talk too wise;*
>
> *If you can dream - and not make dreams your master;*
> *If you can think - and not make thoughts your aim;*
> *If you can meet with triumph and disaster*
> *And treat those two impostors just the same;*
> *If you can bear to hear the truth you've spoken*
> *Twisted by knaves to make a trap for fools,*
> *Or watch the things you gave your life to broken,*
> *And stoop and build 'em up with worn out tools;*
>
> *If you can make one heap of all your winnings*

Naming Ceremonies

And risk it on one turn of pitch-and-toss,
And lose, and start again at your beginnings
And never breathe a word about your loss;
If you can force your heart and nerve and sinew
To serve your turn long after they are gone,
And so hold on when there is nothing in you
Except the Will which says to them: "Hold on";

If you can talk with crowds and keep your virtue,
Or walk with kings- nor lose the common touch;
If neither foes nor loving friends can hurt you;
If all men count with you, but none too much;
If you can fill the unforgiving minute
With sixty seconds' worth of distance run -
Yours is the Earth and everything that's in it,
And - which is more - you'll be a Man, my son!

Acknowledging that a child needs the support of many people in his or her life, and that parents for a variety of reasons cannot always be there, *Gail* and *Alison* have asked *Jessica B* and *Harrison M* to be naming parents for *Barnaby*. The significance and extent of this role is something that has been discussed between them, but naming parents also provide love and support for a child, can be available when the parents cannot, or can be available when the child chooses. It is a unique relationship, sometimes bound by blood and sometimes not, but it acknowledges the role that we all play in nurturing the next generation.

Jessica and *Harrison* – Will your door be open to *Barnaby* when he needs you? Are you each prepared to accept this role in his life, despite the challenges that may present themselves

Dorothy Shorne

as this child comes to terms with life and explores its boundaries?

Jessica & Harrison: We are.

Do you promise that in times of difficulty, *Alison, Gail* and *Barnaby* can turn to you for reassurance and help?

Jessica & Harrison: We do.

Do you promise to keep careful watch over *Barnaby* until he grows to be an adult and to be always ready to advise, encourage and comfort him?

Jessica & Harrison: We do.

Do you promise to offer *Barnaby* friendship without condition and guidance without judgement? Will you share in his successes and support him should he fall?

Jessica & Harrison: We will.

Jessica and *Harrison* have their own offerings to this ceremony today and I invite *Jessica* to step forward to read the poem that she has chosen.

Jessica reads **Isn't My Name Magical**

James Berry

Thank you, *Jessica*. *Harrison* has also considered what advice Barnaby might need today.

> *It is not the critic who counts: not the man who points out how the strong man stumbles or where the doer of deeds could have done better. The credit belongs to the man who is actually in the arena, whose face is marred by dust and sweat and blood, who strives valiantly, who errs and comes up short again and again, because there*

is no effort without error or shortcoming, but who knows the great enthusiasms, the great devotions, who spends himself for a worthy cause; who, at the best, knows, in the end, the triumph of high achievement, and who, at the worst, if he fails, at least he fails while daring greatly, so that his place shall never be with those cold and timid souls who knew neither victory nor defeat.

Theodore Roosevelt, 1906.

Reasonable men adapt to the world. Unreasonable men adapt the world to themselves. That's why all progress depends on unreasonable men.

George Bernard Shaw

To summarise: Be unreasonable and get your hands dirty. By all accounts that's advice Barnaby is already following.

We now come to a special ritual within the ceremony, which demonstrates and strengthens the bonds between parent and child.

If parents are holding the child, he should be passed to a naming parent or other person. Parents are given the taper candles – naming parent to light the candles.

As the parents of *Barnaby*, will you care for him, keep him, clothe him, shelter, and protect him, for as long as he needs you, as best you can? Will you show him by example how to live a life in which he is true to himself and to others?

Gail & Alison: *We will.*

I now ask you to state your specific promises to *Barnaby*.

Dorothy Shorne

Gail & Alison: We promise to respect *Barnaby* as an individual and help him develop his own thoughts and opinions.

We will endeavour to bring *Barnaby* up in a home filled with love and kindness, tolerance of others, respect for humanity and the earth which supports us.

We will commit ourselves to the best of our abilities to provide a secure, loving and caring home that will help *Barnaby* to fulfil his true potential in life.

We promise to nurture a spirit of curiosity, courage and enthusiasm, so that *Barnaby* will not be afraid of life's challenges but can meet them with quiet confidence.

We will always try to offer *Barnaby* unconditional love.

Together, please light *Barnaby's* naming candle.

Gail & Alison light the candle.

The light and warmth from these candles is symbolic of the warmth of your love for your child, and the growing bond between you. Each year at this time, you can relight these same candles, and as the years pass, and the candles become shorter, the love that is expressed in the candlelight about you now will become stronger. May the coming years bless your family with good health, with happiness, and with an appreciation always of your good fortune in each other.

We hereby name you *Barnaby Jet*. We give you your first name – this is the name that sits on your shoulders and reflects your personality. There are many links for this family to the name Barnaby, both geographic and social.

We give you your middle name–this name gives depth and roundness and acknowledges the fact that as a citizen of the world, there will be much traveling in your life.

Naming Ceremonies

We give your family names – these names give you connectivity to those gone before and those still to come. Wear your names with pride and honour.

This Name-giving ceremony will in no way inhibit *Barnaby* from seeking his own truths in life, nor deter him from having any religious commitment or belief. Everyone here is invited and encouraged to present to *Barnaby* as he grows up, a broad and balanced view of life, and despite religious and cultural differences, to embrace the common virtues of integrity, honesty, fairness and concern and love towards all people.

I can see that Barnaby will have many wonderful and positive influences in his life, all of which is so important as described by the following words:

> **Children Learn What is Lived**
> *If children live with criticism, they learn to condemn.*
> *If children live with hostility, they learn to fight.*
> *If children live with ridicule, they learn to be shy.*
> *If children live with shame, they learn to feel guilty.*
> *If children live with tolerance, they learn to be patient.*
> *If children live with encouragement, they learn confidence.*
> *If children live with fairness, they learn justice.*
> *If children live with security, they learn to have faith.*
> *If children live with acceptance and friendship,*
> *They learn to find love in the world.*
>   Dorothy Law Nolte

We are mindful that within each child there exists an immense potential that emerges as the years pass – and we realize with some apprehension that the quality of our own lives will

Dorothy Shorne

determine how well this potential is realized in full bloom and flower. On this day of great promise, we dedicate ourselves to this child, and to all the children who are present.' *Fred A. Cappuccino*

Ladies and Gentlemen – this concludes the formal part of today's ceremony. We are now going to sign the certificates, after which we will drink a toast to *Barnaby* so you might like to take this opportunity to charge your glasses.

Toast: Toast, with a few words from *Gail* and *Alison*.

Naming Ceremonies

No 4 - Abigail Rose

Celebrant rings a small bell three times. Grandmother Annette is holding Abigail.

Douglas and Mira – this is a special ceremony that we share today, and which has importance for all present. We acknowledge firstly your daughter *Abigail* and bring blessings for the great journey that she has ahead of her.

Secondly, we give your daughter her name in this ceremony. In this act we declare that she is an individual, a unique and separate person with a dignity and life of her own. She comes from you, but is separate – a unique individual.

Abigail was born of your love for each other, and through her, you are led into the future. She goes with the support and wisdom of her forebears, and the role of her grandparents and the elders in her life is welcomed. They provide the strength and the certainty of the past, and support you both, as well as helping to guide your daughter.

In bearing a child, you give a tacit undertaking to love, nurture and care for that child, but there are valuable gifts also that you can provide—the gifts of choice and the gifts of freedom. You school them in the understandings of choice wisely, so that they come to learn that there are many choices available to them throughout life: to say yes, or no; to stay or go; to try something different or to walk away. They will be the masters of their destiny. Your gift of freedom, the gift that your parents first gave you, is the freedom for your child to make her own choice. This gift should be bestowed wisely, and you will know when the time is right.

Dorothy Shorne

Frances Cornford, in 'Ode on the whole duty of parents' says the following:

> *The spirits of children are remote and wise,*
> *They must go free*
> *Like fishes in the sea*
> *or starlings in the skies,*
> *Whilst you remain*
> *The shore where they can lightly come again.*

The women in this family will have much to teach the newcomer in their ranks, as she comes of age. *Annette*, maternal grandmother of *Abigail*, I now invite you to speak your wishes for your granddaughter.

Annette speaks and then passes Abigail to Rhonda, paternal grandmother.

Rhonda, Paternal grandmother of *Abigail*, I now ask what are your wishes for your granddaughter.

Rhonda speaks.

Annette and *Rhonda*, thank you to you both.

Douglas and *Mira*, together with your daughter, you are a distinct family unit, but the edges are of that unit blurred for there are many who interact and share with you, be they friends or family. Most of those people are present today, and I wish to acknowledge the importance of your support for this young adventurer both today and throughout her life. There are those who could not actually be here with us, but we acknowledge also their blessings from afar.

Rhonda passes Abigail to Rupert.

Naming Ceremonies

Acknowledging that a child needs the support of many people in his or her life, and that parents for a variety of reasons are not always able to be there, *Douglas* and *Mira* have asked *Rupert*, *Mandy* and *Brayden* to be godparents to *Abigail*. The significance and extent of this role is something that has been discussed between them, but godparents also provide love and support for a child, can be available when the parents cannot, or can be available when the child chooses. It is a unique relationship, sometimes bound by blood and sometimes not, but it acknowledges the role that we all play in nurturing the next generation.

Maggie Dent describes this in her poem, 'The Garden of Life'.

> **The Garden of Life**
> *Children are seedlings in the garden of life.*
> *They need sunshine and warmth*
> *when they are cold and sad;*
> *They need water and nourishment*
> *when they are thirsty and hungry.*
> *They need attention and care,*
> *when they are challenged by life.*
> *And they need to be love, appreciated*
> *and held in awe of their potential,*
> *to be unique, beautiful and like no other.*
>
> *Search for the hero within yourself*
> *and then be there for our kids.*
> *Please feel, listen and care*
> *with your heart and soul and*
> *you will become*
> *a valued gardener in*
> *the garden of life and one day,*
> *a child may hold a special memory of you forever,*

Dorothy Shorne

> *hidden deep in their heart.*
> © *Maggie Dent.*

Rupert, Mandy and *Brayden*—will your door be open to *Abigail* when she needs you? Are you each prepared to accept this role in her life, despite the challenges that may present themselves as this young lady comes to terms with life and explores its boundaries?

Rupert, Mandy and Brayden: We are.

Celebrant rings bell three times.

We bestow upon this young lady her chosen names, selected by her parents with love. She is not named for anyone—this is her own name and one that she can grow into and wear with her own distinctive style and panache. (*to Abigail*) I hereby name you Abigail Rose. We welcome you to this community, and promise you our support as you travel your life's journey, however and whenever you need it. As they have already indicated, your godparents will continue to watch out for you and have the following words of advice:

Mandy: *Abigail*, may you seize the day, whenever and whatever the day. In this, we your godparents support you.

Brayden: Abigail, may you choose your directions in life wisely. When your judgement is wrong, admit it. In this, we your godparents support you.

Rupert: Abigail, may you always be true to yourself. In this, we your godparents support you.

Abigail is passed to Grandfather Peter.

There is a tradition where the grandfather passes a silver coin over the palm of the grandchild. I ask Martin, Abigail's maternal

Naming Ceremonies

grandfather, to perform this tradition, wishing upon Abigail health, wealth, and happiness.

Martin steps forward, takes Abigail's hand, and passes the coin over her palm.

Martin: Abigail, may your pockets be heavy and your heart be light. May good luck pursue you each morning and night. Keep this coin always, and know therefore that you will never be without money.

Abigail is passed to Grandfather Peter.

Celebrant: Grandfather *Peter* has a gift for Abigail which costs little, but is priceless.

Peter: *Abigail*, I give you this box, and inside is a precious stone. It is a stone of your birthplace, and is a reminder always of your roots and your place in this world. Whenever you are lonely or unsure, hold this stone in your hands and draw from its ancient strength and stability.

Celebrant rings the bell three times.

As *Abigail* grows up, she may develop her own spiritual understandings or belief systems, and this ceremony does not intend to pre-empt any such initiatives. It welcomes her into a family where there will always be loving support and stability, and where she will be encouraged to address life's questions and to seek the right answers for herself. She will do so in a nurturing environment, knowing that she has the blessings of those who care for and have confidence in her. *Abigail*, I salute you!

Ladies and Gentlemen – at this point will sign the certificates, during which time you may like to charge your glasses for a toast.

53

Dorothy Shorne

No 5 - Jessica Alice

(Ceremony for an older child)

On the table is a bowl of water, and also a bowl of river pebbles, and a cloak. Guests have been asked to bring a token for Jessica and to pin it on the cloak during the ceremony. A container of safety pins

Family and friends—I welcome you to this place of ceremony, and invite the Goddess to be present in our circle. *Trish and Lee*—this is a special occasion that we share today, and which has importance for all present. We acknowledge firstly your daughter Jessica, and bring blessings for the great journey she has ahead of her. Secondly, we affirm your daughter's names in this ceremony. In this act we acknowledge her individuality, as a unique and separate person with a dignity and life of her own. She comes from you, but is separate, a unique individual.

Your children were born of your love for each other, and through them, you are led into the future. They go with the support and wisdom of those gone before, and the role of Oma and Opa, Heather and James and the elders in their lives is welcomed. Jessica's grandparents relocated to the Barossa a couple of years ago, and have provided support to all members of the family. These people provide the strength and the certainty of the past, and support you both and help to guide your children.

You all are here because of your relationship with this child and her family, for you *are* their community—their circle of people. You are the community with whom they celebrate life's special moments, and to whom they will turn in times of need. Jessica appreciates the role that you all play in her life.

Naming Ceremonies

To be a parent forces you to recognize that you are no longer a child. Claiming adulthood, we look at our children and see ourselves. We feel the temptation to help them succeed where we have failed. But as much as we seek to make them like us, we cannot. What we can do is help them to do their best. As they grow, they will push us to grow with them. This we can do, if we love them not for who they may become, but for who they are—unique. The following poem acknowledges their individuality.

> ***Advice to My Child on Growing Up in Life.***
> *You are unique, my child ... a wonderful addition to life for there is no one else like you.*
> *You are important ... believe it...know it..*
> *Search your heart and be willing to try new things..*
> *Don't be afraid to be different...follow your feelings and be proud...be happy.*
> *Reflect your feelings, your hopes and your dreams...you have much to contribute and other people can learn from you. Take your time...and please, don't hurry.*
> *You must reach out and help others to grow...for the more you give, the more you receive.*
> *Your time on earth is a measure of progress, year by year...for each year will present new and different opportunities.*
> *Enjoy what is beautiful in life, my child, and try to achieve the highest goals in life...to love, to care, to give, to share.*
> *Larry. S. Chengges*

Important friends and role models for Jessica will be siblings Callum and Ronan. They will all develop a special relationship of love and trust with each other, and this will be valued by them always. Trish and Lee are aware of the value of this bond, and are pleased that all their children have mutual support.

Any of you can be people of influence to this girl. It is both a sobering and an inspiring thought. The home, including the extended home, becomes the training ground of future generations, and it will be the way that we relate to our children and life's lessons that we pass on that will influence the type of people they become in the future.

Trish, will you now place a cloak around your daughter.

Cloak is secured around Jessica's shoulders.

Addressing the gathering: You were asked to bring a token today, a token not necessarily of material value but one that Jessica can take with her on her spiritual journey as a talisman of your support for her now and in the future. I ask you to come forward and pin your token to the cloak, and then taking one of these pebbles, to place it in the bowl of water whilst thinking of the wishes that you would bestow upon this child.

Guests come forward one by one, and pin their token on the cloak and place a pebble in the bowl with a wish.

There are others whom *Trish* and *Lee* would like to take an active interest in the welfare and development of their daughter. *Kasey* has been in Jessica's life since the time of her birth, and has always provided love and a deep trustful friendship to the family. *Roger* has demonstrated to Jessica that he is kind, funny, caring, and safe.

Trish and *Lee* ask that you both always welcome *Jessica* if she comes to you for company, advice or help and that you will listen to her and respect her confidences no matter how great or

Naming Ceremonies

small. They ask that you show her understanding and love and let her know she will always have a special place in your heart.

Kasey and Roger - are you will to accept this responsibility to be godparents to Jessica?

Kasey: *I am.*

Roger: *I am.*

Jessica, do you understand that although you can always share aspects of your life with your parents, *Kasey* and *Roger* have agreed to be available whenever you need other caring people in your life?

Jessica: I do.

Kimberley, do you wish to speak on this occasion? (Kim speaks)

We bless this child with the elements of our common being – with earth, air, fire and water.

Celebrant lifts a handful of earth before Jessica and lets it stream through her fingers.

With earth, which is as solid as your given frame, Jessica, we bless you. Take care of yourself as a body, be good to yourself, for you are a wonderful gift. The earth will nurture and support this tree, which grows and matures as you do, bearing you the gift of fruit. Lee, would you assist your daughter in planting the tree.

Lee steps forward and plants the tree with Jessica

Callum waves a long-stemmed flower over Jessica.

With air, which carries the scent of this jasmine flower is as fluctuating as your given passion, we bless you. You will know sorrow and joy, rage and contentment, resentment, and ecstasy. Feel your passions, *Jessica* - they are good gifts.

Ronan steps forward and lights a candle, which will be within a protective glass container.

With fire, which is as illuminating as your given intelligence we bless you. Reason with care, test the world, think with care, for your mind is a good gift.

Trish dips fingers into the wish water and touches them to the crown of Jessica's head.

With water which is as your spirit, my child, we bless you. Grow in conscience, be rooted in good stories. Grow spiritually, for spirit too is a wonderful gift. We now affirm your names of Jessica Alice-.

Celebrant anoints Jessica's forehead with oil.

We anoint you with Bergamot for clarity of thought, Clary Sage for wisdom, Frankincense to give you inner resources and Lavender to heal your wounds and provide soothing. We acknowledge your transition from childhood to adolescence, and hope that you will wear your name with pride, joy, and strength.

Trish has written a poem for her daughter and I will read it on her behalf.

> *Have courage, Dear Heart, when the bearings of love come wandering and illuminates your needs and longings.*
>
> *Have strength, Dear Heart, to learn who you are and stay to thine own self true.*
>
> *Have faith, Dear Heart, when your fears cast a shadow to keep your eyes open and look for the light and find it.*

Have joy, Dear Heart, to find your soul within the melody of song, and dance to your own rhythms.

Have peace, Dear Heart, to stand with your choice made, even if opposition reigns near.

Have awareness, Dear Heart, to speak your truth, even if only your own ears need to hear it, and still like yourself through it.

Be prepared, Dear Heart, to sometimes sit on your fence, holding your own hand in silence.

Above all, Dear Heart, believe in the magic and simplicity that life will bring to you through love, family, friendship, music, food, laughter, truth, and forgiveness,

Knowing in every part of your beautiful soul you are loved now, then and always no matter what.

Patricia J M

This ceremony will in no way inhibit *Jessica* from seeking her own truths in life, nor deter her from having any religious commitment or belief. Everyone here is invited and encouraged to present to *Jessica* as she grows up a broad and balance view of life, and despite religious and cultural differences to embrace the common virtues of integrity, honesty, fairness, concern and love towards all people.

May the circle be open but unbroken May the peace of The Goddess be ever in our hearts. I ask you all now to give your own blessings and congratulations to Jessica.

Dorothy Shorne

No 6 – Roscoe Alaric

(Pagan based ceremony)

Celebrant scatters rose petals in a circle. On a small table in the centre is placed the Naming Candle, two taper candles, a small candle, a bowl of earth, a bowl of water, and the wish box. The guests and parents stand outside the circle.

We have formed this circle of perfect love and perfect trust for the rite of *Roscoe's* Naming, and I call upon the Goddess and God, and all the sacred elements of the Universe to be present in this circle to bless this child. I now ask *Stella* and *Reece* to bring their son into the sacred circle.

My name is Dorothy Shorne. On behalf of *Stella* and Reece I welcome their family and friends here today to take part, in a simple and happy ceremony for their son *Roscoe*. This occasion is also to express to others the thankfulness they feel as his parents.

You will notice that on the table, there is a small box containing some wish papers, and some pencils. Before you leave, you might like to write down your wishes for this child. They will be added to his memorabilia, and when he is able to read them for himself, I am sure he will derive great pleasure from those comments.

To be a parent forces you to recognize that you are no longer a child. Claiming adulthood, we look at our children and see ourselves. We feel the temptation to help them succeed where we have failed. But as much as we seek to make them like us, we cannot. What we can do is see that they do their best. And as they grow, they will in turn be pushing us to grow with them.

Naming Ceremonies

This we can do, if we love them not for who they may become, but for who they are—unique and special.

Stella has the following words of welcome and advice for her son:

Stella to read her own words.

There are many paths in this world and each individual must find their own. Therefore, we have no intention of binding *Roscoe* to any one path while he cannot choose, but rather we ask the Gods and Goddesses, who know all the paths, and who know where each of these paths lead, to bless, to protect and to prepare *Roscoe* throughout his childhood, so that when he is grown, he shall know without doubt or fear, which path is his and he shall tread it happily and successfully.

A Recipe for Dreaming (adapted)

Verse is read.

Bryce Courtney

We bless this child with the elements of our common being – with earth, air, fire, and water.

Celebrant lifts a handful of earth before the child.

With earth, which is as solid as your given frame, my child, we bless you. Take care of yourself as a body, be good to yourself, for you are a good gift.

Celebrant blows gently on the child's head.

With air, which is as fluctuating as your given passion, my child, we bless you. You will know sorrow and joy, rage and contentment, resentment, and ecstasy. Feel your passions, my child, they are good gifts.

Celebrant holds a flame aloft before the child's eyes.

Dorothy Shorne

With fire, which is as illuminating as your given intelligence, my child, we bless you. Reason with care, test the world, think with care, for your mind is a good gift.

Celebrant dips fingers into warm water and touches them to the crown of the child's head.

With water which is as your spirit, my child, we bless you. Grow in conscience, be rooted in good stories. Grow spiritually, for spirit too is a good gift.

Important friends and role models for Roscoe will be his big brothers *Julian* and *Justin* and his sister *Corinne*. The siblings will develop a special relationship of love and trust with each other, and this will be valued by them always. *Stella* and *Reece* are also aware of the value of this bond, and are pleased that *Reece* has *Corinne*, *Justin* and *Julian* to be there for him.

There are others whom *Stella* and *Reece* would like to take an active interest in the welfare and development of their son. *Stella* and *Reece* have chosen four people in whom they trust. These people are friends, sharing fun times and hard times, and *Stella* and *Reece* recognise them to have the qualities of Knowledge, Strength, Love and an open-minded Understanding. They would therefore like them to share these qualities with *Roscoe*.

Stella and *Reece* ask that you always welcome *Roscoe* if he comes to you for company, advice or help and that you will listen to him and respect his confidences no matter how great or small. They ask that you show him understanding and love and let him know he will always have a special place in your heart.

Denise, Al, Paul, and *Karen* – are you willing to accept this responsibility to be godparents to *Roscoe*?

Godparents: We Are

Naming Ceremonies

Paul and *Al*, would you light the two candles held by *Reece* and *Stacy*. *The two godfathers step forward and light the candles.*

Reece and *Stella*, would you now light your son's candle. The light stands for a new life and the hopes you have for Roscoe. The warmth of the flame represents the warmth of human love and friendship. May his life never be dark.

Reece and *Stella*, will you care for *Roscoe*, keep him, clothe him, shelter and protect him, for as long as he needs you, as best you can?

We will.

Will you surround *Roscoe* with affection and love? Will you encourage and support him as he grows up, helping, especially in times of trouble, and making as sure as you can that no harm comes near him?

We will.

We now bestow upon you the names of *Roscoe Alaric*. *Karen steps forward and anoints Roscoe's hands and feet with oil.*

We anoint you with Bergamot for clarity of thought, Clary Sage for wisdom, Frankincense to give you inner resources and Lavender to heal your wounds and provide soothing. We welcome you, and hope that you will wear your name with pride, joy and strength.

This Name-giving ceremony will in no way inhibit *Roscoe* from seeking his own truths in life, nor deter him from having any religious commitment or belief. Everyone here is invited and encouraged to present *Roscoe* as he grows up a broad and balanced view of life, and despite religious and cultural differences to embrace the common virtues of integrity, honesty, fairness, concern, and love towards all people.

Dorothy Shorne

May the circle be open but unbroken. May the peace of The Goddess Be ever in our hearts. I ask you all now to give your own blessings and congratulations to *Roscoe*.

No 7 – Tamsyn Briony and Sylvia Evelyn
(Adolescent Ceremony)

Family and friends – good afternoon. I am Dorothy Shorne, invited as a celebrant to lead this ceremony today. I welcome you to the naming ceremony for Tamsyn and Sylvia, daughters of Alana and Steve. Today's celebration is an official acknowledgement of these two girls, is the occasion at which we formally bestow their names, and is also the occasion of welcoming them into our community.

We are here because of our relationship with these girls and their mother, for we are their community—their circle of people. We are the community with whom they celebrate life's special moments, and to whom they will turn in times of need. We are their extended family and friends and we honour Alana's commitment to her daughters.

To be a parent forces you to recognize that you are no longer a child. Claiming adulthood, we look at our children and see ourselves. We feel the temptation to help them succeed where we have failed. But as much as we seek to make them like us, we cannot. What we can do is see that they do their best. And as they grow, they will in turn be pushing us to grow with them. This we can do, if we love them not for who they may become, but for who they are—unique and special. The following poem acknowledges their individuality.

> ***Advice to My Child on Growing Up in Life***
> *You are unique, my child ... a wonderful addition to life for there is no one else like you.*
> *You are important ... believe it...know it.*

> Search your heart and be willing to try new things. Don't be afraid to be different...follow your feelings and be proud...be happy.
> Reflect your feelings, your hopes and your dreams...you have much to contribute and other
> people can learn from you. Take your time...and please, don't hurry.
> You must reach out and help others to grow...for the more you give, the more you receive.
> Your time on earth is a measure of progress, year by year...for each year will present new and different opportunities.
> Enjoy what is beautiful in life, my child, and try to achieve the highest goals in life...to
> love, to care, to give, to share.
>
> *Larry. S. Chengges*

Tamsyn is ten years old and Sylvia is nine, so both have had time to get used to the names that we will bestow on them today. This ceremony takes place, not at their birth and initial introduction to the world, but at the time of their movement towards adolescence. This is a time when some of the patterns and behaviours of childhood are ready to be discarded, and instead they will be seeking new patterns and acceptance, and embracing new responsibilities and roles. It is only natural that those to whom the girls will turn to for role models will be those with whom they have closest contact – their parents and family, and close friends and associates.

Any one of you can be people of influence to these girls, particularly at this important time of transition. It is both a sobering and an inspiring thought. The home, including the extended home, becomes the training ground of future

Naming Ceremonies

generations, and it will be the way that we relate to our children and life's lessons that we pass on that will influence the type of people they become in the future.

Tamsyn and Sylvia also have older sisters in Alice and Sonia and they will be important role models, as in turn will Tamia and Sophia be for their younger brother, Bodhi. The bonds between siblings can be so important through life. Grandparents also have a special role in passing on cultural values to their grandchildren. They can assist children to find their identity and their inner security and to integrate themselves into society. Acknowledgement is given to Susan and Matthew Montague, and Daisy and Phillip Larson, grandparents to Tamsyn and Sylvia.

Alana has chosen friends Graham M. and Katie S. to be Godparents and mentors to Tamsyn and Sylvia. They will provide the girls with advice and support as they grow up. I ask that you always welcome the girls if they come to you for company, advice or help and that you will listen to them and respect their confidences no matter how great or small. Angela asks that you show her daughters understanding and love and let them know that they can always come to you in time of need.

Graham and Katie – are you willing to accept this commitment towards Tamia and Sophia?

Graham & Katie: We do.

Tamsyn and Sylvia, do you understand that Graham and Katie are people who are trusted by your mother to take an interest in your lives, and who will be there for you if you need help or advice, or just simply someone to talk to? We do.

We now come to a special ritual within the ceremony, which demonstrates and strengthens the bonds between parent and child. Graham, could you please light the candle that Alana is holding.

Alana is given her candle – Graham to light the candle.

Alana – as a parent, you already have a strong commitment towards your daughters. Do you promise to Tamsyn and Sylvia that you will provide them with a loving and caring home, will allow them the freedom to develop their own personalities, and will endeavour to give them a strong sense of identity and self-esteem? Will you teach them the value of kindness, tolerance, and honesty, as they grow and develop into young women? I will.

Tamsyn and Sylvia—will you give your mother the same respect that she gives you, talk to her when there are things to discuss, help her in times of need, and learn to love her in time, not just as a mother but as a friend?

Tamsyn and Sylvia: *We will*.

Alana, will you please light your daughter's candles from the one that you hold.

Alana steps forward and lights the candles.

The light and warmth from these candles is symbolic of the warmth of your love for your daughters, and the growing bond between you. Each year at this time, you can relight these same candles, and as the years pass, and the candles become shorter, the love that is expressed in the candlelight about you now will become stronger. May the coming years bless your family with good health, with happiness, and with an appreciation always of your good fortune in each other.

Are you ready to receive your names? Each be proud of your name, and make it proud of you. Graham, will you now please

Naming Ceremonies

sprinkle Tamsyn and Sylvia with the petals. We now bestow upon you the names of Tamsyn Briony and Sylvia Evelyn. May life's blessings fall on you as do these petals here today. We wish you happiness and fulfilment in your life. You may now blow out the candles.

For both of you, we hope that you learn to trust in the essential goodness of those around you, and that through the advice and guidance of those who have promised to care for you today, that you develop the confidence of young people who have never had reason to doubt their worth. The words of the following poem are my final advice.

> *Always believe in yourself*
> *Get to know yourself –*
> *What you can do and what you cannot do –*
> *For only you can make your life happy.*
> *Believe that by working, learning and achieving*
> *You can reach your goals*
> *And be successful.*
> *Believe in your own creativity*
> *As a means of expressing*
> *Your true feelings*
> *Believe in appreciating life.*
> *Be sure to have fun everyday*
> *And to enjoy the beauty in the world.*
> *Believe in love.*
> *Love your friends, your family,*
> *Yourself and your life.*
> *Believe in your dreams*
> *And your dreams can become reality.*
> *Susan Polis Schutz*

Dorothy Shorne

I now ask Katie to assist with our final blessing today. Katie will you sprinkle the magic dust over the girls, with these words:

Katie: With this magic dust, you are empowered to create your own destiny with love, fortitude, respect and honour. May it also bring health, happiness, and good humour.

This Name-giving ceremony will in no way inhibit Tamsyn and Sylvia from seeking their own truths in life, nor deter them from having any religious commitment or belief. Everyone here is invited and encouraged to present a broad and balanced view of life to the girls as they grow up, and despite religious and cultural differences, to embrace the common virtues of integrity, honesty, fairness and concern and love towards all people.

Thank you for your attendance and your good wishes towards Tamsyn and Sylvia today. We will now conclude the ceremony with signing of the documents.

No 8 – Zachary Daniel

Family and friends, my name is Dorothy Shorne and I have been asked to officiate on this special occasion. Graham and Karen feel pride and joy in the arrival of their son Zac and take this opportunity to formally introduce him to you, their family and friends, and to confirm and bestow upon their son his chosen names.

You will notice that on the table, there is a pile of papers, and some pencils. Before you leave, you might like to write down your wishes for this child. They will be added to his memorabilia, and when he is able to read them for himself, I am sure he will derive great pleasure from those comments.

Becoming a parent is both a wonderful and indescribable feeling. Graham and Karen have chosen to have a naming ceremony because they want the opportunity to express in their own way, the love and commitment they have to Zac.

Graham and Karen also take this opportunity to acknowledge the assistance that Linda has given, in not only driving down from Pt Pirie to be here, but who was also roped in to help with organising the day.

Graham and Karen have undertaken to nurture this child, to love him, provide him with a safe and secure environment, with stimulation, and with guidance as he plots his own course through life. Zac is an individual, and as such his future path will be uniquely his. Graham and Karen will be there with him throughout, to love and support him, however and whenever he needs it.

An important friend and role model for Zac will be his big brother Jason, whom I had the pleasure of meeting on a similar

Dorothy Shorne

occasion some years ago. Though no doubt there will be typical sibling rivalry, Jason will develop a special relationship of love and trust with his little brother, and this will be valued by them always. Graham and Karen are also aware of the value of this bond, and are pleased that Zac has Jason to be there for him, as big brothers are very special people.

As an assertive young adventurer, making a foray upon the world around him, Zac has a child's trusting confidence in his ability to do what he wants. The full extent of what he can do may be frustrated by his parents, who may impose justifiable limitations but as he grows, we need to foster that innate belief in his abilities, with a little wisdom thrown in as well.

> *Always believe in yourself*
> *Get to know yourself –*
> *What you can do and what you cannot do –*
> *For only you can make your life happy.*
> *Believe that by working, learning, and achieving*
> *You can reach your goals*
> *And be successful.*
> *Believe in your own creativity*
> *As a means of expressing*
> *Your true feelings*
> *Believe in appreciating life.*
> *Be sure to have fun everyday*
> *And to enjoy the beauty in the world.*
> *Believe in love.*
> *Love your friends, your family,*
> *Yourself and your life.*
> *Believe in your dreams*
> *And your dreams can become reality.*
>   *Susan Polis Schutz*

Naming Ceremonies

Zac you are too young now to understand, but with love and caring and through example, your parents will explain to you the difference between right and wrong, the concept of sharing and the meaning of love. They will also support you as you learn to laugh, to grow, to look, to listen and learn. It is an enormous responsibility for them, but a joyous task as well.

Children are a social responsibility. Many of us here today are possibly not parents, but we are aunts and uncles, neighbours, and friends. In a myriad of little ways and by example, we are all teachers and mentors. The rewards are not always immediate or obvious, but like all long-term investments, the initial input of time, patience, understanding and caring example will give an ultimate return of a balanced and responsible human being – plus with a few warm fuzzy feelings as interest along the way!

Graham and Karen are helped in this respect by Zac's grandparents Ray and Tessa Ramsay, and Gemma and David Brown as well as the godparents they have selected. Gemma and Dav Brown are very disappointed at not to be able to attend. They had planned to be here, but Dave was involved in a car accident last week and wasn't able to make the journey from Pt Pirie. We wish him well in his recovery.

Godparents take a special interest in the ethical, material, and moral development of the child. It is a serious responsibility, but one that can be more rewarding, and we come now to this important part of the proceedings where I address this question to the godparents.

Sharon Greentree and *Kurt Magee* – you have been asked to accept the privilege of becoming godparents to *Zac*. *Graham* and *Karen* ask that you always welcome *Zac* if he comes to you for company, advice or help and that you will listen to him and respect his confidences no matter how great or small. They ask that you show him understanding and love and let him know he will always have a special place in your heart. Sharon and Kurt, are you willing to accept this responsibility to be godparents to *Zac*?

Godparents: We are.

Graham and *Karen* – as the parents of Zac, will you care for him, keep him, clothe him, shelter and protect him, for as long as he needs you, as best you can? Will you show him by example how to live a life in which he is true to himself and to others?

Graham & Karen: We will.

Jason, could you come forward and light *Zac's* Naming Candle.

We now bestow upon you and confirm your name of *Zachary Daniel*. It is a name that you have been using for some time now, and just as names develop associations according to the people that we know, the name *Zac* has come to signify a little person with a 'can do' personality, someone who is not going to be left behind and who pushes his way through life with a certain determination.

The name *Zachary* was chosen simply because *Graham* and *Karen* liked it, but *Daniel* was chosen in honour of *Zac* and *Jason's* big brother *Daniel Liam*, who sadly died several years ago. *Jason* and *Zac* now each bear one of their brother's names. May you bring joy to your parents, your godparents, your big brother, and to all of us, your family and friends. May you join us in striving to make this world a better and happier place.

Naming Ceremonies

These are challenging times in which we live, and who knows what developments and innovations will occur in the lifetime of this young man? The words of A A Milne pose some interesting questions.

> *Where am I going? I don't quite know.*
> *Down to the stream where the kingcups grow –*
> *Up to the hill where the pine-trees blow –*
> *Anywhere, anywhere. I don't know.*
> *Where am I going? The clouds sail by,*
> *Little ones, baby ones, over the sky.*
> *Where am I going? The shadows pass,*
> *Little ones, baby ones, over the grass.*
> *If you were a cloud and sailed up there,*
> *You'd sail on water as blue as air,*
> *And you'd see me here I the fields and say:*
> *'Doesn't the sky look green today?'*
> *Where am I going? The high rooks call:*
> *'It's awful fun to be born at all.'*
> *Where am I going? The ring doves coo:*
> *'We do have beautiful things to do.'*
> *If you were a bird, and lived on high,*
> *You'd lean on the wind when the wind came by,*
> *You'd say to the wind when it took you away:*
> *'That's where I wanted to go today!'*
> *Where am I going? I don't quite know.*
> *What does it matter where people go?*
> *Down to the wood where the bluebells grow –*
> *anywhere, anywhere. I don't know.*

Ladies and Gentlemen – at this point we are going to sign the certificates, following which we will drink a toast to *Zac*

Dorothy Shorne

and his future. You might like to take this opportunity to charge your glasses.

Signing of the documents

I now ask you to all raise your glasses in both a toast and a welcome to *Zac Daniel*. With these our best wishes, you *Zac* are empowered to create your own destiny with love, respect, fortitude, and honour.

To Zac!

❊

Sections of any of these ceremonies may be mixed and matched, or used as the framework for an entirely new ceremony. If desired, parents may like to add a few words of their own either as an introduction or at the end.

Baptism Ceremony

It would normally be expected that a civil celebrant would perform a secular ceremony, that is a civil or naming ceremony, and that if parents wish their child to be christened or baptised, then it would be done in the church of their choice. Sometimes, this baptism is not possible and it may be for a variety of reasons. Perhaps be that the parents do not particularly wish to align themselves with any particular church, but still would like to welcome their child into God's community.

There are 'freelance' Christian celebrants who will perform this ceremony, and some civil celebrants are also comfortable with the religious components. Another option is that the civil celebrant performs the ceremony with another participant who may deliver the religious blessings or passages.

Under the teachings of most churches, anyone can baptise or christen a child, although it is commonly a religious celebrant using the format required by their particular doctrine. Should there be a situation of urgency, and should there not be a religious officiant available, then anyone can baptise the child. In that situation and assuming that the child survives, the baptism may be ratified later within a church service.

The format commonly used would incorporate:

' NN I baptise you in the name of the Father, and of the Son, and of the Holy Spirit.'

The sign of the cross may be made on the child's forehead, with holy water, if available. Such water is created 'holy' through blessing.

The example given is not meant to replace a religious ceremony, nor does it purport to baptise a child into a particular church. Rather it would be used when the parents of a child wish to recognise their religious or spiritual beliefs and to welcome their child into not only their family and social circle but to acknowledge that child as part of God's wide community.

It is an adaptation of both a baptism and a naming ceremony, and of course as with all ceremonies can be further modified by both parents and celebrant to meet the needs of any given ceremony or belief. A Baptismal Certificate can be presented to the child instead of a Naming Certificate. Prayers may also be incorporated within the ceremony, and a civil celebrant may find it appropriate to ask a member of the family or other guest to lead the prayer.

I am the light of the world; he who follows me shall not walk in darkness, but shall have the light of life.
John 8:12

Naming Ceremonies

Baptism Ceremony - Jacob Tyrone

Family and friends -my name is Dorothy Shorne, and I have been asked to officiate on this special occasion and I invite you all to join me in celebrating the Baptism of this child.

Martin and *Louise* have been blessed with a beautiful baby son. They wish to express their joy on the birth of Jacob. They are pleased that he has arrived safely into this world and want to welcome Jacob into their family unit, to the wider family of friends and relatives and to the community of the Lord. The presence of God and those gathered here today is appreciated, as will be your interest and involvement in the years ahead.

The Gospel words of Mark tell us of the response of Jesus to little children.

> *They brought children for Jesus to touch. The disciples rebuked them, but when Jesus saw them he was indignant and said to them, "Let the children come to me; do not try to stop them; for the kingdom of God belongs to such as these. I tell you, whoever does not accept the kingdom of God like a child will never enter it." And he put his arms round them, and blessed them.*

Louise would like to express in her own way the significance of parenthood for her.

> ***A Tribute to Jacob***
> *As parents we would like to welcome*
> *our baby son into our lives.*
> *Our precious little boy is a gift from God*
> *who guided us and answered our prayers*
> *in conceiving Jacob.*

79

Dorothy Shorne

> *God will assist us to take care of him*
> *in good and bad times.*
>
> *Jacob has filled our hearts with, joy, laughter*
> *and lots of happiness. He is a good-natured*
> *adorable little fellow, and we will promise*
> *to love, honour, and cherish him and to provide a good*
> *caring family home for him. To the best of*
> *our ability we will teach, clothe, feed our son*
> *and give him love and a moral upbringing.*
> *We ask God to bless him with good health,*
> *faith, happiness, luck, confidence and strong*
> *self-esteem that will protect him from Evil,*
> *and enable him to intuitively help others in Life.*
>
> *If he is troubled at any time in his life, and*
> *finds it hard to approach us, he can then*
> *seek support and advice from his Godparents*
> *Sandra and Shane, or help from other*
> *Family members in solving his problems.*
> *Communication is the key in reaching understanding and*
> *solution.*
>
> *Written with Love by his parents Martin & Louise.*

Martin and *Louise* will be there for *Jacob* throughout his life, to love and support him, however and whenever he needs it. There are others who will take an active interest in the life of this child, and I now ask *Sandra, Jacob's* Aunt to read a prayer written by Rudyard Kipling.

> **Teach Us**
> *Father in Heaven who lovest all,*
> *O help Thy children when they call;*

That they may build from age to age
An undefiled heritage.
Teach us to rule ourselves always;
Controlled and cleanly night and day;
That we may bring, if need arise,
No maimed or worthless sacrifice.
Teach us the strength that cannot seek,
By deed or thought, to hurt the weak:
That, under Thee, we may possess
Man's strength to comfort man's distress.
Teach us delight in simple things,
And mirth that has no bitter springs;
Forgiveness free of evil done,
And Love to all men 'neath the sun!
                    Rudyard Kipling (1865-1936)

Jacob has been blessed with grandparents. They have a special and privileged role to play in the life of their grandson. Although he has his parents as primary carers, it is just as important that there are others to whom a child can look for guidance. This is where grandparents become very important people and we acknowledge the value of their influence.

Grandparents pass on cultural values to their grandchildren. They can assist children to find their identity and their inner security and to integrate themselves into society. Acknowledgment is given to *Jacob's* Grandparents, *Bob* and *Sue S* and *Roland* and *Mary M*. As his Grandparents, we ask you to share your experiences in life with *Jacob*. Love received from Grandparents is without conditions and is developed within a relationship that can have more freedoms than that between parent and child. It is very important to allow *Jacob* to feel loved and needed by more than just his parents, and we thank you for welcoming him into your lives as you have done.

There is a tradition where the grandfather passes a silver coin over the palm of the grandchild. I would like to ask *Roland* to step forward to perform this tradition, wishing upon Jacob health, wealth, and happiness.

(Roland steps forward and passes a silver coin over the palm of his grandchild.)

Celebrant: Godparents have a direct role to play in the life of *Jacob*. An important and traditional part of today's ceremony is the commitment about to be made by the people chosen by *Martin* and *Louise* to fulfil a special role for *Jacob* – to be his godparents.

Celebrant: *Shane* and *Sandra* - Do you promise that in times of difficulty, *Martin, Louise* and *Jacob* can turn to you for reassurance and help? Do you promise to keep careful watch 0ver *Jacob* until he grows to be an adult and to be always ready to advise, encourage and comfort him?

Shane & Sandra: We do.

From the beginning of time, men and women have brought their children to the houses of worship for dedication. In the presence of the congregation, the child is given his name and the parents declare their responsibility for him. We have chosen to meet here in this beautiful garden, knowing that all around us is the results of God's creation and as such we stand in the Garden of the Lord. We acknowledge the mystery of the power that is in us and works through us, and we are humble before that mystery.

We give the child a name in this ceremony. In this act we declare that the child is an individual, a unique and separate person with

Naming Ceremonies

a dignity and life of his own. He comes from us, but he is not ours. He is himself, an individual. In giving him a name we declare that we will respect him as himself, and give him the freedom to be himself.

We perform this ceremony publicly to declare that all of us, as parents and as representatives of society, are responsible for the care and development of all children. It is our task to give them a world of peace and justice in which to grow. It is out task to give them our ideals and hopes. By presenting the child to the gathering, the parents acknowledge that the child is more than a private possession, but is a new being in whom we all have a responsibility, and whom we all welcome to the community.

We use a flower and water – time-honoured symbols – in this ceremony. They remind us of the beauty and wonder and freshness of life. We dedicate ourselves to the task of nourishing the beauty and wonder and freshness of this child, and all children. 'Whether a flower comes into full bloom or not; whether it fulfils itself as a flower or not – depends on the nurture it receives. No flower grows alone, apart from the sunshine and the rain, apart from the soil in which it lives. So, too, no child grows alone.'[1]

Shane, would you now step forward and light your Godson's Naming Candle.

To Jacob: We now bestow upon you the names of *Jacob Tryone*. We wish you a long life and happiness, in a loving and peaceful world. May you bring joy to your Parents, Grandparents, Godparents, and to all of us, your family and friends. *Sandra*, would you please sprinkle some magic dust over your godson:

Dorothy Shorne

With this magic dust, you *Jacob* are empowered to create your own destiny with love, fortitude, and honour. The future is yours and you have the power to influence the outcome. Use your skills wisely, and know that there are those who love you and from whom you can always seek guidance and support.

This ceremony will in no way inhibit Jacob from seeking his own truths in life, nor deter him from having any specific religious commitment or belief. Everyone here is invited and encouraged, despite religious and cultural differences, to embrace the common virtues of integrity, honesty, fairness, and love.

On a lighter note, you may like to hear some thoughts on just what is a boy?

A Boy

After a MALE baby has grown out of long clothes and nappies and has acquired pants, freckles, and so much dirt that relatives dare not to kiss it between meals, it becomes A BOY.

A boy is nature's answer to that false belief that there is no such thing as perpetual motion. A boy can swim like a fish, run like a deer, climb like a squirrel, balk like a mule, bellow like a bull, or act like a jackass, according to climatic conditions.

He is a piece of skin stretched over an appetite; a noise covered with smudges. He is called a tornado because he comes at the most unexpected times, hits the most unexpected places, and leaves everything a wreck behind him. He is a growing animal of superlative promise, to be fed, watered, and kept warm.

Boys faithfully imitate their dads in spite of all efforts to teach them good manners. A boy, if not washed too often, and if kept in a cool, quiet place after each accident,

will survive broken bones, hornets, swimming holes, fights, and nine helpings of pie.

A boy is a joy forever, a periodic nuisance, the problem of our times and the hope of a nation. Every boy born is evidence that God is not yet discouraged with man.

Rev. Leo Fahey

It is appropriate that we draw this ceremony to a close with a blessing, in acknowledgement of *Jacob's* place in this world, or the influence of his parents, and of the love of God.

Celebrant to place hand lightly on child for the blessing

Remember O God your child *Jacob*, that as he grows in knowledge of your truth, he may be led to acknowledge your truth in his life.

And continue to bless O Lord the parents of this child, that they may be strengthened to keep the promises they have made, and so to live that *Jacob* may see in them what it is to live a good and sound life.

I invite those here who will continue to share *Jacob's* life with *Martin* and *Louise*, to bless him also. Gently, we will pass him between you so that you may have your own moment with this child, warming him with your good wishes before passing him to the next person.

Dorothy Shorne

We now conclude the formalities of the day with the singing of the Certificates.

Naming Certificates

The person named receives a Naming Certificate as part of the ceremony. Other certificates are available as well. Templates for certificates are available in the **Naming Ceremony Workbook**.

Several Naming Certificates designs are available.
Also:
Appointment as Godparent
Appointment as Guardian
Appointment as Mentor
Appointment as Fairy Godmother
Thank you to my Parents
Thank you to my Grandparents
Thank you to my Great Grandparents
Thank you to my Brother
Thank you to my Sister

Certificate of Namegiving

I, Dorothy Shorne hereby certify that I have this day in the presence of the undersigned Witnesses at Parish Vineyard, Leasingham, South Australia Celebrated the Namegiving for

SOPHIE VIOLET WHITE

Who was born on the Tenth day of May, 2018

Mother .... *Paul White*

Godparent .... *Sue Smith*

Dated this Tenth day of May 2018

Father .... *Rob White*

Godparent .... *Peter Beadel*

Celebrant .... *Dorothy Shorne*

Certificate of Namegiving

I, Dorothy Shorne hereby certify that I have this day in the presence of the undersigned Witnesses at 34 Rugby Street, Oaklands Park, New South Wales Celebrated the Namegiving for

ELLIOT MICHAEL GRAYSON

Who was born on the Twenty Seventh day of January, 2014

Mother .... *Naomi Grayson*

Godparent .... *Stephen Owen*

Dated this Twenty Seventh day of January 2014

Father .... *Shane Grayson*

Godparent .... *Kelly Tomesi*

Celebrant .... *Dorothy Shorne*

Naming Ceremonies

Thank you to my Grandparents

Grandparents, with a lifetime of experience behind them, and freed from the daily struggle for survival which characterises the early years of marriage, bring a unique and special love, understanding, and guidance to the grandchild who has the good fortune of access to them...." **Thomas Davidson**

This is to certify that on the Nineteenth day of January 2013

at Underwood Park, Rostrevor, South Australia

I celebrated the namegiving for

ALICE EVELYN FISHER

An essential part of this ceremony was the appreciation and recognition given to

Selina and Colin Cashen as Grandparents.

Signature of Celebrant

Dorothy Shane

Rites of Passage 0411 228 164

Certificate of Appointment as Godparent

This is to certify that on the Twentieth day of July 2012
at 43 Rogerson Crescent, Harbourside, South Australia

Katherine Smith was appointed Godparent for

CHARLIE IAN POSSINGHAM

Thank you from _____

Mother   Father   Celebrant

Rites of Passage 0411 228 164

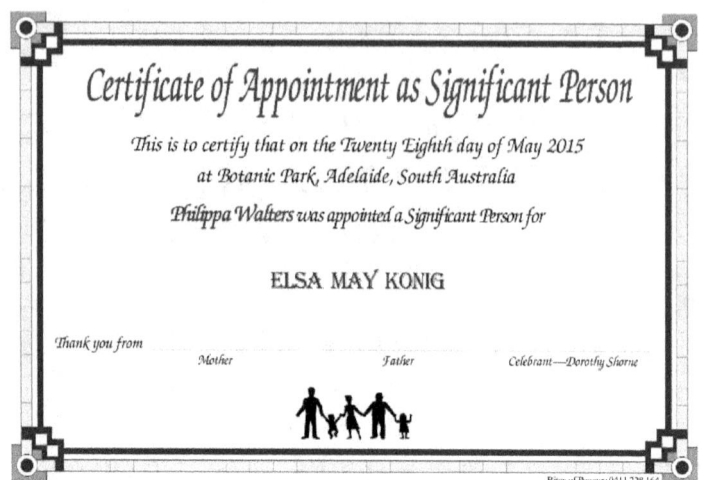

Suggested Readings and Verses

Through Baby's Eyes.
I didn't expect a brass band,
With welcome mat unfurled,
To be on hand when I arrived,
In this confusing world.

Nor did I expect a doctor,
To hold me by the feet,
Then quickly turn me upside down,
And spank me on the seat.

At first I wasn't quite prepared,
For this enormous place,
Nor for the funny characters,
That I would have to face.

But I soon learned to get my way,
By looking sweet and shy,
And when I wanted to be held,
To make a fuss and cry.

I've found it really doesn't take,
Much difficulty or guile,
To wrap them round my finger,
All I need to do is smile.
Edgar A Guest

Dorothy Shorne

A Thought to Ponder On
The heart of a child is a garden,
Where new plants take root day by day,
And many the seeds that are sown there,
So carelessly tossed by the way.
Each seedling is watered and nourished,
And furnished a climate to grow,
And those who have part in a child's life,
Are planting and nourishing so.
How seriously we must consider,
Our words and our actions always,
Lest we plant and nourish a bad seed,
In some child's heart garden today.
   Henry Wadsworth Longfellow

Look to this day, for it is life.
Look to this day,
For it is life, the very life of life.
In its brief course lie all the
Varieties and realities of your existence:
The bliss of growth,
The glory of action,
The splendour of beauty;
For yesterday is but a dream
And tomorrow is only a vision,
But today well lived makes
Every yesterday a dream of happiness,
And every tomorrow a vision of hope.
Look well therefore to this day!
Such is the salutation of the dawn.
  From the Sanskrit

Naming Ceremonies

Twins
So many good things come in pairs,
Like ears and socks and panda bears.
But best of all are sets of twins,
With extra laughter, double grins.
There's so much fun in having two
With twice as many points of view.
So much alike, forever linked,
And yet they're also quite distinct.
They share a birthday and a name,
But moods and tempers aren't the same.
Although at times they may dispute,
Their loyalty is absolute.
From days of youth till life is done,
It's one for both and both for one.
We're all quite novel and precise,
But special folks God made twice.
Larry Howland

A Tribute to All Daughters
Every home should have a daughter
for there's nothing like a girl,
To keep the world around her
in one continuous whirl.......
From the moment she arrives on earth
and on through womanhood,
A daughter is a female
who is seldom understood.....
One minute she is laughing
the next she starts to cry,
Man just can't understand her
and there's just no use to try.....
She is soft and sweet and cuddly
but she's also wise and smart,
She's a wondrous combination
of a mind and brains and heart.....
And even in her baby days

Dorothy Shorne
she's just a born coquette,
And anything she really wants
she manages to get...
For even at a tender age
she uses all her wiles,
And she can melt the hardest heart
with the sunshine of her smiles.....
  Helen Steiner Rice

What is a Girl?
She's an angel, she's a princess
She's a sweetheart, she's an elf.
She's a pint sized little dear
who wants to do things for herself.
She's a busy little lady
with so much to see and do
That she's usually into everything,
which keeps you busy too!
She'll always be "Dad's little girl"
and "Mum's best helper", too
As all the joy she brings your way
keeps growing each year through.
  Richard Henry Stoddard

A New Baby Boy
As your eager arms reach out
to hold this child you've dreamed about,
You will feel consuming joy
in knowing you've produced a boy.
The pride you feel in your son
will gain in strength as time goes on.
God grant your baby vibrant health,
may happiness provide his wealth,
so that your home will always stay
the happy home it is today.
  Helen Steiner Rice

Children

Your children are not your children.
They are the sons and daughters of life's longing for itself.
They come through you but not from you,
And though they are with you, yet they belong not to you.

You may give them your love but not your thoughts,
For they have their own thoughts.
You may house their bodies but not their souls,
For their souls dwell in the house of tomorrow,
Which you cannot visit, not even in your dreams.
You may strive to be like them, but seek not to make them like you.
For life goes not backward nor tarries with yesterday.
You are the bows from which your children
as living arrows are sent forth.

The archer sees the mark on the path of the infinite,
And he bends you with his might that his arrows may go swift and far.
Let your bending in the archer's hand be for gladness;
For as he loves the arrow that flies,
So he loves also the bow that is stable.

Kahlil Gibran

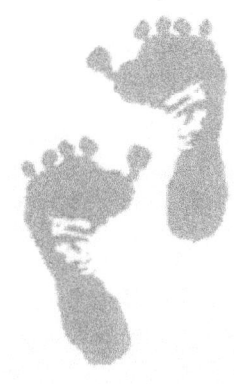

Dorothy Shorne
A Reading
Each second we live is a new and unique moment of the universe, a moment that will never be again. And what do we teach our children? We teach them that two and two make four, and that Paris is the capital of France.

When will we also teach them what they are?

We should say to each of them: Do you know what you are? You are a marvel. You are unique. In all the years that have passed, there has never been another child like you. Your legs, your arms, your clever fingers, the way you move.

You may become a Shakespeare, a Michaelangelo, a Beethoven. You have the capacity for anything. yes, you are a marvel. And when you grow up, can you then harm another who is, like you, a marvel?

You must work -we must all work -to make the world worthy of its children.
Pablo Casals

Prayer for Boys
God bless all little boys who look like Puck,
With wide eyes, wider mouths, and stick-out ears,
Rash little boys, who stay alive by luck,
And Heaven favours, in this world of tears.
The thousand question-asking little boys,
Rapid of hand, and foot, and thought as well,
Playing with gorgeous fancies, more than toys,
Heroes of what they dream, but never tell.
Father, in your vast playground, let them know
The loveliness of Ocean, Wood, and Hill.
Protect them from every bitterness and woe,
Your heedless little acolytes, and still
Grant me the Grace, I ask upon my knees
Not to forget that I was one of these.
Arthur Guiterman

Oliver James Rupert

He's the child I always wanted
He's the source of my delight,
But he's the reason that I haven't slept
for many a disturbed night.
My social life is waning
and money runs out through the door,
And keeping up with all his needs
is such a thankless chore.

I knew he would be demanding,
that life would never be the same,
but I didn't know that Mother love
is just another name
for yet another pile of washing –
smeared breakfast on the floor,
apple cores behind the cushions
and felt pen scribbled on the door.

And just when I think, 'I've had enough,
I cannot handle this!'
a little hand creeps into mine,
and he gives a sloppy kiss.
That little smile that's full of love
reminds me what I've done.
I chased my dream, I clung to it,
And now, I have my son.

I can't describe the feeling
as we get to know each other;
shared looks and laughs and secrets
are the joy of any mother.
Good fortune and fortuity
have looked on us and smiled.
I cannot now imagine
what life would be without this child.
Dorothy Shorne

Dorothy Shorne

A Boy

After a MALE baby has grown out of long clothes and nappies and has acquired pants, freckles, and so much dirt that relatives dare not to kiss it between meals, it becomes A BOY.

A boy is nature's answer to that false belief that there is no such thing as perpetual motion. A boy can swim like a fish, run like a deer, climb like a squirrel, balk like a mule, bellow like a bull, or act like a jackass, according to climatic conditions.

He is a piece of skin stretched over an appetite; a noise covered with smudges. He is called a tornado
because he comes at the most unexpected times, hits the most unexpected places, and leaves everything a wreck behind him. He is a growing animal of superlative promise, to be fed, watered and kept warm.

Boys faithfully imitate their Dads in spite of all efforts to teach them good manners. A boy, if not washed too often, and if kept in a cool, quiet place after each accident, will survive broken bones, hornets, swimming holes, fights, and nine helpings of pie.

A boy is a joy forever, a periodic nuisance, the problem of our times and the hope of a nation. Every boy born is evidence that God is not yet discouraged with man.

Rev. Leo Fahey

A message to every adult

When you thought I wasn't looking, I saw you hang my first painting on the refrigerator, and I immediately wanted to paint another one.

When you thought I wasn't looking I saw you feed a stray cat, and I learned that it was good to be kind to animals.

When you thought I wasn't looking, I saw you make my favourite cake for me and I learned that the little things can be the special things in life.

When you thought I wasn't looking I heard you say a prayer, and I knew there is a God I could always talk to and I learned to trust in God.

When you thought I wasn't looking, I saw you make a meal and take it to a friend who was sick, and I learned that we all have to help take care of each other.

When you thought I wasn't looking, I saw you give of your time and money to help people who had nothing and I learned that those who have something should give to those who don't.

When you thought I wasn't looking, I saw you take care of our house and everyone in it and I learned we have to take care of what we are given.

When you thought I wasn't looking, I saw how you handled your responsibilities, even when you didn't feel good and I learned that I would have to be responsible when I grow up.

When you thought I wasn't looking, I saw tears come from your eyes and I learned that sometimes things hurt, but it's all right to cry.

When you thought I wasn't looking, I saw that you cared and I wanted to be everything that I could be.

When you thought I wasn't looking, I learned most of life's lessons that I need to know to be a good and productive person when I grow up.

When you thought I wasn't looking, I looked at you and wanted to say, "Thanks for all the things I saw when you thought I wasn't looking."

Dorothy Shorne

Each of us, parent or friend, influence the life of a child. How will you touch the life of someone today?

Mary Rita Schilke Korzan

The Velveteen Rabbit

"In the children's book, the Velveteen Rabbit, the young rabbit asks the Skin Horse, who has been round the nursery for some time, what is real, and does it hurt. "Sometimes," said the Skin Horse, for he was always truthful. "When you are real you don't mind being hurt."

"Does it happen all at once, like being wound up," he asked, "or bit by bit?" "It doesn't happen all at once," said the Skin Horse. "You become. It takes a long time. That's why it doesn't happen often to people who break easily, or have sharp edges, or who have to be carefully kept. Generally, by the time you are real, most of your hair has been loved off, and your eyes drop out and you get loose in the joints and very shabby. But these things don't matter at all, because once you are real you can't be ugly, except to people who don't understand."

Getting real is about embracing and accepting your authentic fully expanded self, it takes in all your parts - the selfish, scared, and cruel along with the expansive and tender - the bad and the good. It frees you to seek the truth about yourself more vigorously, to see the world in a truer perspective. It gives you courage to take the new steps, to experience an even deeper, stronger marriage, to find greater satisfaction in work and pursue more fulfilling friendships. These are the things we wish for you."

Margery Williams

Searches either on the internet or at your local library will reveal many other potential readings. I have only published here those that are no longer subject to copyright, or for which I have permission from the author.

When you do use the work of another person, acknowledge them as the author of the piece.

Dorothy Shorne

Organising the Celebration

Naming celebrations are generally informal and casual affairs, as one would expect for an occasion that is usually attended by many small children. Typically, they are hosted in parks or a family home, though occasionally at a small function centre or restaurant instead.

Parks are ideal for picnics, and usually have playgrounds for the children. The children tend to entertain each other, although under the supervision of an adult (swing pusher). Of consideration in choosing this venue is the availability of picnic benches and seating, and the amount of food and other chattels that must be carried from the car. As there are often many family groups using parks, be sure to give your celebrant very precise instructions on how to find you.

Using the family home (or that of a relative or friend) means that kitchens, toilets, bedrooms, and changes of clothes are easily on hand. It is a familiar and usually safe environment, and is more easily controlled, particularly in case of adverse weather. The down-side is the cleaning up after the event, but for a relatively casual affair, this should not be too onerous.

Some Naming Ceremonies are followed by lunch, and others by afternoon tea. The actual timing of the ceremony may depend on the age and routine of the child. This tends to be more successful after the guest of honour has had the right quota of daily naps, and has been fed. The ceremony is therefore timed to coincide with a happy, contented, and clean child.

Small babies often go to sleep during the ceremony; toddlers may want to sit at your feet and keep playing. They may want their best mate to stand with them as well. Flexibility is essential in any situation involving young children. It is practical if the ceremony is not too lengthy, as there may be a limited time frame of concentration and good humour in which to deliver it. Fifteen minutes would usually be the maximum time to spend on the ceremony for a young child.

The celebrant will need access to a small table or area on which to place the Naming Register and certificates for signing, and any items used during the ceremony such as candles, rose petals, water, etc. Be sure to clarify with the celebrant which items you should supply.

Guests tend to be more casual about punctuality for Naming Ceremonies, sometimes because they have small children themselves and domestic organisation is a challenge, and sometimes because they do not appreciate the importance of arriving in a timely manner for these events. Invite guests for a time at least half an hour before the time the ceremony is to commence, and ensure that they understand that a celebrant has been engaged to deliver a ceremony at a precise time.

Besides naming and welcoming the newcomer, Naming Ceremonies are a great way to foster community and kinship with your friends and family. It can be a rewarding experience for all involved.

Dorothy Shorne

Acknowledgements

I wish to thank the following for permission to publish verse, poetry, or portions of ceremonial text.

Jim Boswell, *Thankfulness for a special child*
Maggie Dent, *The Garden of Life*
Larry Howland, *Twins*
Mary Rita Schilke Korzan, *When you thought I wasn't looking*
Dally Messenger, *Ceremonies and Celebrations*

Further Reading:

Baby Blessings, June Cotner,
Bless This Child, Edward Searle
Ceremonies and Celebrations, Dally Messenger
essential love, Ed Ginny Lowe Connors
Great Occasions, Ed. Carl Seaburg
New Arrivals, Jane Wynne Willson, British Humanist Assoc
Saving our children from our chaotic world, Maggie Dent
Seasons of Life, compiled by Nigel Collins

'*Saving our children from our chaotic world*' is available directly from the author Maggie Dent at www.esteemplus.com.

Also By Dorothy Shorne

Rites of Passage Series

From This Day Forward
It's Your Funeral
Naming Ceremonies
The Last Farewell

Fiction

Skywalkers

Writing as Emily Hussey

Red Centre Series
Tales from Harrow Series
Sandy Bay Series
Maison Angelique
Ambition and Passion

About the Author

Dorothy Shorne has had a varied career. She built modular houses in Central Australia on remote aboriginal settlement, opened various businesses, and was involved in the development of Sydney Airport when it was operated by the Federal Airports Corporation.

She was a marriage celebrant for 24 years, and has married couples in different locations, ranging from private gardens, to beaches, to caves, or rural locations. Many of her clients remain friends to this day. She usually writes with Iris, a black and white cat at her elbow, demanding her share of attention. Writing tends to be fueled with regular coffee boosts, and occasional squares of very dark chocolate.

❀

Under the name of Emily Hussey, she is a published romance writer, and loves the short story format in a range of genres. Dorothy now resides on the coast in the city of Adelaide, and is exploring the writing options in every café in walking distance.

❀

Contact Details: dorothy@shorne.com.au.
Any comments are welcome, and if you leave a review at the place where you purchased this book, I would be delighted.

www.ingramcontent.com/pod-product-compliance
Lightning Source LLC
Chambersburg PA
CBHW072014290426
44109CB00018B/2234